BRAT

Grateful Steps Foundation
159 South Lexington Avenue
Asheville, North Carolina 28801

Copyright © 2015 by Alan Marshall, Ph.D.
Library of Congress Control Number 2014914573

Marshall, Alan
Brat: Diary of an Ego State

Cover illustration modified by Michele Scheve
from original work of David Helwer
Angry boy on cover: "Boy Injured," licensed from iStock
Sweet boy on cover: photography by Petr Kratochvil
Back cover photograph of Jake and Dr. Marshall by Kristen Marshall

ISBN 978-1-935130-95-6 Paperback

Printed in the United States of America
Lightning Source
FIRST EDITION

www.gratefulsteps.org

Preface

This is a book about dissociation. Lots of frogs experience a process similar to it. Many varieties have the ability to survive ten years or more without water or food. They simply remain underground in a moribund state, where their hearts beat about once an hour, and then suddenly revive full strength when the rains come. What the frogs undergo isn't precisely the same as dissociation but has some points in common. Primarily, it is a survival strategy, just like dissociation. It's not an illness—it's instead a way of suspending life until circumstances are more favorable for living. Like dissociation, it means missing out on a lot of what happens during those years, but it's better than missing out altogether. We find these kinds of frogs amazing. I think dissociation is equally amazing, and often just as life preserving.

Though dissociation is similar, there are some important differences. Dissociation in humans is very similar to physical shock. If a person is seriously injured or in some way severely traumatized, his or her body may shut down many of its normal operations in order to direct blood flow toward purely life-sustaining activities. The individual may even lose consciousness for a period of time, or go into a coma. Then, when the trauma is past, the body can gradually go back to routine functioning. If asleep, the person can return to full wakefulness, and often be able to recall much of what caused the shock reaction in the first place.

Human dissociation usually does not involve dramatic changes in body function such as redirection of blood flow. Instead, when the pain of the trauma becomes too much to bear the person becomes partially unconscious. It is then that the magic happens: somehow, a different part of the brain takes over the intolerable portion of the pain, so that the person is temporarily spared from experiencing it. There is no "willing" this to happen; it is purely reflexive. Indeed, in some people, there is no way to stop it from happening. In cases of severe trauma, this can literally save the person's life—and often his or her sanity. Like the frogs, there are now things that the person has missed out on, but that hopefully can be brought back to awareness when the time is right. That's what therapy is for.

This book is my conceptualization of what happens inside the mind of someone who dissociates regularly, a condition I call Ego State Disorder. This is similar to Multiple Personality Disorder (or what is currently diagnosed as Dissociative Identity Disorder), but is a milder form of it. There are a number of questions addressed:

1. How does an Ego State, or Part, come into existence?
2. Is it instantaneous?
3. Where does it come from?
4. Does it bring with it parts of the host person's consciousness, knowledge, skills?
5. Can Ego States, see, hear, smell and feel things?
6. Can they think new thoughts?
7. Can they learn?
8. Can they exchange ideas and memories with each other?
9. Do they ever become fully integrated?
10. Can the so-called disorder be "cured"?

I've addressed most of these questions in the book, although the "answers" require some deduction on the part of the reader. The last two deserve some additional comment. For #9, I suppose it is possible for the Parts to become fully integrated, though I have never seen, nor heard of it happening. As different ones become aware of the legitimacy of the others, and the factual nature of their memories, the conflicts among them lessen, and the person has less tension and more energy for living. In fact, the person can then actually call on some of the resources of the various Parts in daily life.

The response to #10 is similar. If these things occur, what need is there to even discuss "cure"? I think the idea is a hangover from the days of the "Medical Model" in psychology, where diagnoses were used to describe "what is wrong with you," and treatments were supposedly adjusted according to those diagnoses. But saying Ego State Disorder is "what is wrong with you" is simply not helpful in my view. As I implied above, I don't really think of this as a "disorder." I'd prefer the word "adaptation," or possibly "adjustment." It seems to me a means of preserving sanity—and often life itself—instead of losing it. Needless to say, people who experience a great deal of dissociation are often left with certain liabilities in our society. They usually think and feel differently than most people, and so feel considerable isolation. I believe most of them are above average in intelligence, sensitivity and creativity, which—sadly—leads to increased isolation. They also seem more likely to be open to paranormal experiences. The main "problem" they have is, I believe, more psychological (and sometimes physical) pain than most people. That's what drives them into therapy.

Much of what is in the book I have witnessed firsthand, but there are exceptions. For example, I have never witnessed different Parts actually conversing with each other or having direct contact in any way. But I believe at some deep level that we are not privy to, contact does occur once the barriers between the Parts are broached.

It is also important to realize that the two Ego States described in this book are unique, and not to be thought of as "typical" in any regard. There seems to be an almost infinite variety of Ego States and Alters (the latter being the separated parts of Multiple

Personality Disorder). Even though there are countless numbers of them out there, it is probable no two are exactly alike. The one writing the diary herein comes into existence entirely outside the awareness of the host person and remains undiscovered for much of his life. It is usually a shock to anyone to discover such a thing, and the issue needs to be approached with sensitivity. The notion that there are forces operating within us that we are unaware of is odious indeed, not to mention frightening.

There is one underlying assumption of this book that needs explicit mention, and that has to do with the nature of the Unconscious. In my judgment, it is a repository of many things that have been driven out of consciousness, mostly traumatic memories. If those memories would simply sit there and be quiet, it would be one thing. But that is not what happens. Instead, the memories have a primal impetus to push forward until they are once again conscious. Presumably, the human brain has evolved in this direction for some good reason, and it seems to have to do with healing. The more repressed material there is in the unconscious, the more the person has to work to maintain the suppression. The more that material can be cleared out, the more energy the person has for his everyday life.

Prognosis is essentially a guessing game. As I say in the text, there is usually no one-to-one correspondence between catharsis/ insight and improvement in one's life. At the same time, I have witnessed a good number of occasions where there did seem to be a close connection, so that overall the matter is very unpredictable.

Some people seem to know at an early age that therapy is necessary for them. Others seek it out only when the psychological pain becomes unbearable. Likewise, some people seem to benefit from it more than others, and some not at all. So prognosis is essentially a guessing game. All the therapist can do at the outset is try to establish a solid connection with the patient and allow the healing process to begin.

Alan Marshall, PhD.

BRAT
Diary of an Ego State

Alan Marshall, Ph.D.

Grateful Steps
Asheville, North Carolina

Chapter One

It happened in a flash. Uncle Ted was using his huge fists to beat up little Norm (the kid I used to be part of), and it got so bad Norm started to pass out. Then suddenly here I am, taking the beating instead of Norm! He isn't really asleep, but I can tell he's not feeling the pain anything like I am. And when the beating is over, he doesn't remember it nearly like I do. So he managed to get away from part of it, which I guess is a good thing. Except that now *I'm* stuck with it! What's fair about that? I mean, it's not really supposed to be *my* pain—I sure didn't do anything wrong! So of course the first thing I do is try to give it back to Norm, where it belongs. That's when I see for the first time—*he still can't stand it!* So he starts to pass out all over again. I actually tried a second time, hoping a little rest would make a difference. No luck. He starts grabbing his head and moaning, and I hate so bad seeing him in that kind of misery that I give up. But not forever. I may have to hold this for him for a while, but it *ain't* gonna be permanently. Like I said, I didn't do anything wrong, and I'll be danged if I'm going to suffer like this for no good reason. But there's another thing that's more important: I want to be back inside Norm! Truth is, he's me, and I'm him, and I don't think either of us will ever be happy with things being this way. But I'm beginning to realize this is going to take time. I'll have to find some other way to get the memory and the pain back to him or things will never be right.

That beating happened several years ago, and there were many more beatings afterward. The same thing happened almost every time: Norm could stand it up to a certain point, and then would start to pass out, and then I had to take over. Why? Why did I have to take over? Dammit. Just because he couldn't stand it, and I didn't want to see him die. At least it seemed like that's where it was headed. Seems like it was just a sort of reflex, and neither of us seemed to have had any choice in the matter. And all these years later I *still* haven't figured out a way to resolve it. I wish there were some way to just dump this pain overboard, so we didn't have to deal with it at all. But that's not the way it is.

Now that I'm thinking back over this stuff, I have a bunch of questions. How long is this going to take? Is it ever going to get better? How do I know how to write? How do I know to even be asking these *questions*? Danged if I know. The bottom line is, though, none of it matters a whole lot. What matters is this unbearable pain. How am I going to get rid of it, and get back where I belong? The aloneness just makes it all that much worse. Luckily, I get some relief from it when I'm sleeping, and I do that a lot! So there is a bunch of Norm's life I miss out on. When I'm awake, I'm just always on the alert for an opening to get back to him, even though it means I have to restore the pain to him. Like I said, so far I've had very little success. As soon as I begin and he starts the moaning and grabbing his head, it hurts me even worse—seeing him go through it all over again. I wish I didn't care. It seems like it would all be easier. But I *do* care! After all I'm *part* of him, and I *miss* him! But as far as the pain—he's older now, and tougher, and it seems like he should be able to stand it better. But that doesn't seem to be true. Still, I *can't quit trying.* That's the one thing I know for sure.

To sum up, life in here is pure hell. I feel like I'm stuck in a deep dark dungeon somewhere with no chance of ever getting out. There're only two things I can do: one is try every chance I have to get back to Norm, and the other is write in this diary. I have to keep it away from him, at least for now. I know if he ever read it, the pain would start coming up too fast all over again, and I'm sure he would just put a match to it. I don't even really know why I'm writing it, except it gives me something to do.

ENTRY 2:

Quite a few years have passed. I never can tell exactly how many, being asleep so much of the time. But I think Norm is an adult now, so I guess I am too. But I sure don't *feel* like an adult. I still feel like a little kid, and one with a helluva chip on his shoulder. I've come close to giving up on being with Norm many times, and have become very cynical. I don't trust anybody—guess I never really have. But all this aloneness and the constant pain has made me more miserable than ever. I actually feel like I'm ugly, and somebody Norm would never like even if I could somehow get back to him. And even though I know I'll never give up, I sure wish I could.

This all didn't start out so terribly. Norm and his sister, Maggie, seem to have had a great start in life. They had super parents who loved them and took really good care of them up until they got killed in a car accident. Norm was four and Maggie was seven when they got sent to live with their father's brother, Ted, the guy I mentioned above. He was a real terror. Ted was married to Sadie, who wasn't so bad to us kids. But she was terrified of Ted, so she did nothing at all to stop the beatings. I showed up a few years later, like I said, during one of the worst. Ted was grinding his knuckles into the top of Norm's head so bad it was tearing out chunks of his hair. Not enough of it so you could see the bald spots clearly, or the teachers at school would have been asking questions. Ted was clever that way. And he never did that to Maggie for some reason. I never could figure that one. The physical pain wasn't the only thing. The other was the hate. Ted seemed to *hate* Norm, at least from the time I showed up. It was so severe I had to take on the worst of that also. So naturally I wound up hating Ted just as much as he hated Norm. Finally, when Norm was sixteen, it all built up to the point where I came flying out during one of the beatings and actually beat *Ted* up! I can't begin to tell you how good it felt. I still remember the look in his eyes, like "Where did YOU come from?" I know Norm was sore as he could be for days afterward and didn't really remember all of what happened. But the good thing was that Ted never touched him after that. Not one time. In fact, he kind of stayed out of arm's reach, like he was a little afraid of what might erupt out of Norm. Namely, *me!*

ENTRY 3:

Norm just had his thirtieth birthday, but there was no celebrating. Things have gotten really bad around here. His wife, Kelly, went on and on about how she was sick and tired of his bad moods and how they always came on when he was drinking. It's not like he ever hits her or the two boys, Jake and Paul. But I know he does get real mean. And it's partly my fault. When he has a few beers, he stops having to be the nice, thoughtful guy he is all the rest of the time, and it gives me an opening to do you-know-what. I get an opportunity to be my feisty self. Not that it ever accomplishes much, but like I said before, I can't quit. If Norm had to live every day with this level of misery he'd do the same thing, I'm sure. *Any* of them would, I bet. But the way it is, Norm has no idea why he gets so angry, and none of them have any idea I'm even here at all, let alone causing so much of this. There, I did it again: said *I* was causing it. But I know perfectly well it isn't *me* causing it! I'm actually the one trying to *fix* the nightmare created by Ted. But there's no way to do that without bringing up the pain, and of course everybody hates that, and so they hate me—or at least they would if they knew I was here and what I'm trying to do. So the whole thing is one big mess, and I'm just plain worn out with it.

Anyway, recently Kelly's been threatening to leave, and saying the only way she'll agree to stay is if Norm gets some help. Whatever that means. So he's called this doctor, and is going to see him tomorrow. Needless to say, I'll be right there with him, in case this guy tries anything funny. Doctors don't scare me any more than his boss, or Kelly, or anybody else for that matter. He'd just better watch his step.

ENTRY 4:

Here's the first session:

> DOC: "What brings you here?"

> NORM: "My wife. And I guess me, a little bit. She's tired of me yelling at the kids, and not paying her any real attention. At least that's what she says. Also says I'm

real changeable, and she never knows how to react to me."

Doc: "And what about *your* 'little bit'?"

"Well, I do sort of know something's wrong. The kids really don't deserve to be yelled at. At least not for little things. It just comes out of my mouth before I can stop it. I've told myself a thousand times to quit, and it does no good at all. And as for Kelly, there's a problem: I think I care more about her than gets out in the open. I sometimes want to tell her about it, but I just can't squeeze it out. So there're some things I *can't* say, and other things I can't *stop* from saying. Dammit anyway."

Doc: "So, bottom line, are you here for yourself, or just because your wife is forcing you?"

"It's mostly her. For myself, I gave up on changing years ago. I've tried everything I know, and nothing has helped. I mean, you seem like a nice enough guy, but what are you supposed to do that I haven't already done?"

Doc: "All I can suggest to you is to give this therapy a try. At least for a few weeks."

That was about it. I could tell Norm wasn't the least bit hopeful. And, of course, neither was I. The Doc seemed okay to me. Talked halfway straight and let Norm say his piece. I guess Norm'll give it a shot for a while.

ENTRY 5:

Next session:

NORM: "I had a dream last night I thought I ought to tell you about. Something about a prison, or some real dirty, awful place. Seemed to be a lot of conflict and uneasiness. I couldn't tell who was involved—it was just a feeling. That's all I can remember."

DOC: "I think you told me last time that Kelly claims you have some very different moods. Did I recall that right?"

"Yeah. She's said I almost seem like different people at different times. I'm pretty sure she's exaggerating. She does that sometimes."

DOC: "But I'm guessing she knows you pretty well. Doesn't she?"

"Yeah. Real well. Maybe too well. I don't like it when she senses something going on that I haven't even told her about.

A little spooky. Like she's psychic or something. But anyway, what's wrong with having different moods?"

Doc: "Maybe nothing. Can you tell me what they're like?"

"Well, most of the time I'm the same. Pretty laid-back, maybe a little quiet. And then there are times the quiet part really takes over, and I don't want to say anything, or have anybody say anything to me. I think underneath that is a feeling of deep distrust and cynicism. But then I can be real nice too. And then of course there's the anger. Sometimes it really does get out of control. That's when I start yelling. Mostly at the kids, but occasionally at Kelly. I really hate that because I know she doesn't deserve it. And neither do the kids. That's the one thing I'd like to work on, if you have any idea of how to go about it. Do you?"

Doc: "I can't promise you anything. But I think so, yes. And I think your dream has given us a starting point. I would guess the 'uneasiness' and 'conflict' in the dream might have to do with different 'states of mind,' as well as just moods. Those are not the same. They usually are the result of painful events in your past. Are you aware of any things that caused you a lot of physical or psychological pain?"

"Well, yeah. But I'm not sure if it's anything too unusual. My parents were killed in an auto accident when I was four. They were the best. Me and my sister, Maggie, were about as happy as any two kids could be. Then we both got sent to Uncle Ted and Aunt Sadie's to live, and things turned awful. He was a violent drunk, and she was a worthless nobody who did nothing to stop him."

Doc:"Stop him from what?"

"Oh, just . . . stuff. I don't remember much about the details, but I know it was bad. Maggie says it was *real* bad, but she doesn't talk about it much. Now *there's* somebody who should get some help. She weighs about 80 pounds, is 5 feet 7 inches tall, and looks like a pitiful refugee. She won't stop exercising, and eats almost nothing. Swears she's fat. Never married, won't even date. Says nobody would like a fat woman like her! I know she's not crazy, but I worry about her all the time. She won't even consider therapy."

Doc: "Sounds to me like she went through some pretty terrible things, to wind up like that. You say she doesn't talk about it much, but it's possible she doesn't even remember a lot of what happened that was so bad. Does that sound like a crazy idea to you?"

"Now wait a minute. I thought they disproved all that—the 'False Memory Syndrome' or something."

Doc: "No doubt there are such things as false memories. For example, for years I believed I remembered some things from my own past that I later discovered could not have really happened. But I also know from my own therapy there were things I had repressed that were extremely helpful to me when they finally resurfaced. And I see the same thing with patients on a regular basis."

"So you mean you were a wacko too? You needed therapy yourself?"

Doc: "Yes, indeed. I'm a lot like you. I could have made it through life without any help, but I would have been half a person, and miserable much of the time. I'm very glad I did it. It was what made me decide to become a therapist myself."

"Okay, I can accept that. But let's get back to these 'states of mind,' if that's what these really are. How do we go about changing them?"

Doc: "First I need to tell you they are not all that easy to change. Moods, as you know, can change in a few seconds. States of mind, however, are more enduring, since they involve attitudes and perceptions which have become more stable over long periods of time. An example might be your feelings about religion. Those have formed over your lifetime and are not easily changeable. Nonetheless, it *is* possible to have more than one 'state of mind' about religion. Part of you might feel strongly, for example, about the existence of God, whereas a more 'scientific' part might have serious doubts. From what the dream tells us about your internal conflicts, and what Kelly has said about them, they might be very central to what we're working on here. If it turns out they're just moods, that's not much of a problem. But if they really are different states of mind, they are probably causing you a good bit of internal conflict and confusion. I just think it's an important possibility to keep track of."

That was about it, but it scared me pretty bad. Seems to me Norm is starting to *trust* this guy! How stupid can he get? I may have to come up

13

with a dream that will bring him back to his senses.

ENTRY 6:

It seems to have gotten through, and Norm started out with it in the next session. "I had another dream during the week. That's pretty odd in itself. I hardly ever remember what I dream."

Doc: "It's actually fairly common for people to recall more dreams when they're doing this work. I'd urge you to try to remember as many as you possibly can."

Norm: "Well, in this one a guy was skating along on some rollerblades when he lost his balance and fell hard. A guy in a white coat showed up and pretended to help, but grabbed him too hard and made the pain worse. Then the white coat disappeared, and the guy wound up having to take care of everything himself. What do you make of that?"

Doc: "I think the most important question is what do *you* make of it?"

"To tell the truth, I couldn't help but think of what you and I are doing. I'm here because of being in trouble, and you're the one in the 'white coat' who's supposed to help. But then you don't. You leave, and I'm on my own again. I feel bad saying that, but it's what occurred to me when I woke up."

Doc: "I promise you, you needn't feel bad about it. Every single person who's walked through that door has had similar feelings of anxiety and distrust. They all, including you, have good reason to feel that way because of what they've experienced. All I can tell you is I'm not leaving, and I think you'll find you *can* trust me. But that takes time, and it's not fair to ask you to go faster than feels right to you."

Well, that dream didn't work like I thought it would. This Doc character is pretty smooth, but I can outsmart him. I'm not letting Norm get squashed again like so many other times. I've seen him just act like a happy little kid sometimes, trusting just about everybody, like he forgets all about being beaten and lied to and hated. Right up until the axe falls for the fiftieth time. We're not going there again, not if I can help it.

ENTRY 7:

I would swear Norm seemed almost anxious to get to the next session. It went like this:

"I talked with Maggie last week after our session. I asked her some questions about our early lives, and I could hardly believe her answers, meaning: there were almost none! It's like she didn't remember much of *anything!* No wonder she doesn't ever want to talk about those times. Makes me think whatever happened to her was even worse than my stuff."

Doc: "I'm really sorry to hear that. I hope like you do, that she'll find a way to get some help. But getting back to the task at hand, I have an idea. One way to start exploring forgotten memories is by way of hypnosis. Have you ever tried it?"

"No, and the thought gives me a bad feeling. What are you proposing?"

Doc: "Not anything where you lose control or I take it over. None of that. The way we'd go about it, you would be conscious enough the entire time to tell me the moment you wanted to stop. And I *would* stop. No questions asked.

It's basically a one-time technique, just used to give us both an idea of what sorts of things we might be headed for. And after that, we would probably not use it again. I would encourage you to think about it during the week and let me know next session."

Well, this made me even more scared. Doc seems to be moving awfully fast, trying to get Norm sucked in to remembering everything. Doesn't he know I've tried that for years, and it just winds up in disaster? Norm seems to trust him way more than he should. I'm hoping I can fix that.

ENTRY 8:

I could tell Norm wasn't nearly as eager to show up this time. Pretty scared. Asked Doc a lot of questions about what was going to happen. Finally he consented to try the hypnosis. He lay back on the couch and closed his eyes.

Doc: "Okay, like I told you, I'm just going to count down very slowly from ten to one, and I want you to concentrate on your breathing. Don't do anything at all to change it—just pay attention to it. Try to learn as much about what your body is doing as you can, as though you were going to be quizzed about it later. Here we go . . . ten. . . nine . . ."

By the time he got to one, I could tell Norm was very relaxed. I knew that could be an opening for me. I decided if they were really going through with this nonsense, at least I'd try to get rid of a little of this blasted pain I'm stuck with.

Doc: "Now try to let me know if you see any images or notice anything the least bit unusual. Even if it's something like smells or odd bodily sensations."

Norm, after several minutes: "This makes no sense at all. I'm seeing a real dark place, like a long hallway. No, wait . . . it's not a hallway . . . more like a dungeon. Reminds me of that dream I had. Cell doors on one side. Can't make out anything clearly." Long silence. "It's almost like I can hear somebody down there, like they're crying."

Doc: "Can you tell what the crying is about?"

"Not really. It's very soft. But it's definitely crying. Ooh, ouch!" Norm grabbed his head. "Okay that's enough of this." He opened his eyes and sat up.

Doc: "That looked very painful. What happened?"

"My head! Felt like it was going to explode. Happened all of a sudden. Totally unexpected. First I'm seeing this weird dungeon, and then I get whacked. Now what is all that supposed to mean?"

Doc: "Well, it's too early to be sure. I don't know if you realized it or not, but you grabbed the very top of your head. Not the place for a typical headache. Have you had pain like that before?"

"Yes. Many times. I may have forgotten to tell you, but it's been a problem for about as long as I can remember. Always right on top of my head. It's still hurting, but it's starting to fade now. But what in the world is that dungeon about?"

Doc: "*Whatever* it's about, I'm pretty sure it's important. When you saw it, do you remember what you were feeling?"

"Yeah. Creepy. It was not a nice place. And the crying didn't help."

Doc: "Okay. I know it's not obvious, but I think we found part of what we were looking for. Once again, you might want to pay particular attention to your dreams. That, and see if there is anything more that comes to mind about the dungeon. It sounds to me like there are things going on in there we need to know about. Also, try to pay attention to your body. A lot of times the pain we experience in the present is connected with things from long ago that we've forgotten."

On the way out the door, Norm added, "One other thing: the crying sounded familiar. There are times when Kelly is getting on my case, and I wind up crying in a way that sounds a lot like that. At least that's what she says. Myself, I fade out some and don't hear it real clear. I know it's a bit childish, but I can't seem to help it. She hates it! I just can't seem to get a handle on it, and she has no patience with it at all."

Doc: "I'm glad you told me that. I think it's important."

Well, some of the pain got out, all right. I just hope Doc got a peek at how bad this might be! But there's something I don't get: where was the crying coming from? Sure as heck not *me*. Nobody makes me cry. Not Doc, not Ted—nobody. But Norm could hear it, and strange as it seems, I could too! Does that mean there's somebody down here besides me? Come on, now—I don't need things more complicated than they already are!

ENTRY 9:

When Norm got home after the session, Kelly asked what had happened. Said he looked awful. He couldn't seem to talk about it and went right to the fridge for a beer. She got really mad. Said that was his way to escape everything, to drink it away. Then he did something I've only seen him do a few times—he drew his arm back like he was going to hit her! Scared me to death! I'm sure it did her also. She picked up her car keys and left the house. After several hours, she finally came back, but she was still furious. She told him if he ever hit her—even once—the marriage was over. I could tell by her voice she wasn't kidding, and Norm knew it.

Then he changed again! Something made him apologize over and over and swear it would never happen again. His voice got real soft, and he was crying, just like he does sometimes. A lot like in the therapy session. For some reason I could tell this was not the regular Norm. It's not that I'd never seen this before, but I guess after hearing Doc talk about it and hearing it myself in the session, I noticed it more. Kelly noticed it too. Made her even madder! She asked him who the hell he was. Said she'd seen this act a million times and was sick of it. That he'd apologize and feel so bad about what he did and then just turn around and do it again the next chance he got.

Once again I couldn't help wondering about the crying in the session. It sure sounded a lot like what's going on here. Where the devil is it coming from?

Somehow, in the midst of all this, Norm kind of shook himself and managed to look Kelly right in the eyes and tell her he really was sorry, that he'd told Doc about these times, and they were working on it as hard as they could. It took her a few minutes, but she softened and said she was very glad to hear that. I'd never seen that happen before. It makes me wonder if maybe the therapy is making him change a bit. But truth is, I doubt it. I'm not near as easily fooled as he is.

ENTRY 10:

I lost a good bit of time since the last session. Norm and Kelly are still together, although things are very tense. She demanded that he give the therapy at least another month, and he agreed. The next session went like this:

DOC: "So you say things are worse at home?"

NORM: "Yeah. I really blew it after the last session. She wouldn't leave me alone about it, and . . . well . . . to tell the truth, I wanted to hit her. It just erupted in me like it does sometimes, and I lost control. Not only that, but later on I turned into a bawling baby. I couldn't stop crying, and I apologized a dozen times and swore I'd never do it again. She got even more pissed, and said she didn't know who I was, and she'd seen that act a thousand times, and it was pure BS. There was one good thing, though. Somehow I managed to snap out of it partly and tell her I truly was sorry and that you and I are working on it. I think she believed me."

DOC: "I'm really glad to hear that. But have you ever actually hit her?"

"No, not quite. But I've come real close. She said if I ever did, we were done. I can't let that happen, Doc! I know I'll never find anyone like her again. Dammit, I DO need help. Or am I maybe already beyond it?"

DOC: "No, not at all. But there's something we need to find out. These moods of yours seem to be extremely powerful. And the sudden switch to being babyish is something we need to address."

"Yeah, I guess so. How do we do that?"

Doc: "Let me tell you what I'm thinking. Remember my telling you about 'states of mind'? Another term for those is 'Ego States.' Sometimes when a person suffers a lot of trauma, his mind splits into parts. It's like they're different parts of the brain. I'm not talking about the 'Alters' of Multiple Personality Disorder where there are completely separate personalities. Ego States are not entirely separate but have some of the same qualities. I'm not sure whether you have these Ego States or not, but there's a fairly easy way to find out. Do you want to know?"

"No. I mean yes. I don't guess I really have any choice. Ego States, demons, whatever. Let's find out what the hell is wrong with me."

Doc: "Okay. If they're in there, they're usually holding painful memories for you, which they want to get rid of by bringing them to the surface and into your consciousness. All I have to do is ask if they're in there, and some of them will usually be anxious to communicate with us in some way. Do you want me to try?"

After a lot of fidgeting, Norm said: "Let's give it a shot. I suppose I need to close my eyes."

Doc: "Right. Now, this is a bit like hypnosis, so you might want to try to relax. They can't always respond in words, but if they're there, you'll 'know' it." Doc takes a deep breath. "Okay, here we go. I'm pretty sure those of you inside, if you're there, have heard what I've been saying. You also know Norm has not known about you previously in any direct way. This is your chance to let him know *if* you're there. Just one thing now—GO SLOW. Don't blow him away."

Can you begin to imagine my turmoil? On the one hand, it seemed like, after all these years of having to stay hidden, Doc was inviting me to come right out into the open! But it was just too much. How did I know he wasn't going to reject me just as soon as the pain started up, just like Norm had forever and ever? I got all twisted up inside with hope and dread and couldn't resist what happened next. I came flying out, and made Norm holler, "YOU go slow! Or better yet, you GO AWAY!"

I expected Doc to just shrivel up and end the session. But somehow he responded calmly:

"First, whoever you are, I want to thank you for coming forward. I know that's not so easy. Second, I want you to know I understand what you're saying. Therapy does sometimes make things worse in the short run, and this seems to be one of those times. But if you can find a way to work together with us, I think Norm will be much better off. I want to go back to adult Norm for right now, but I want you to know you're entirely welcome here. That goes for you and anyone else who might be in there with you. I'm not kidding about that. Norm, I can see you're shaking, and I don't blame you at all. This is hard stuff to digest."

Norm shook his head so I thought it might fall off, and finally said: "I don't know why that stuff came out of my mouth. I'm sorry. It was *really ugly*."

Doc: "I didn't see it as ugly at all. I thought it was the truth. Part of you has good reason not to trust me, based on everything you've been through in your life. That Part, or Ego State, is trying to protect you. It really believes that I, and the therapy, might be damaging to you, and it has the courage to say so. I see it as a good friend of yours, and I think in time you will also."

"Whatever you say, I suppose. All I know is I feel like the whole earth just turned on its axis, and I have no idea what is up or down or who the hell I *am*. I mean, never in my life have I completely lost control like that. It really did feel like I was demon-possessed, and the demon had way more power than me. I don't think I like this one little bit. To tell you the truth, it scares me to death!"

Doc: "I know. The main thing I want you to know right now is you're not crazy. Plenty of perfectly normal-appearing people have Parts like this, but most of them have no idea about them. I think you'll find, in time, they *are* your friends, and can help a lot in the therapy process. They can fill in a lot of the blanks in your memory, so your life will make more sense to you. But I know perfectly well right now those are just words. You're still the same person you've always been, but now you have the possibility of knowing yourself a lot better. And maybe even *feeling* a little better on top of it."

When Norm got home, I guess he still looked like he'd been hit with a brickbat. Kelly said, "Whoa! What's going on here?"

Norm opened his mouth to say something, but nothing came out. He just sputtered, and then started crying again! Somehow, I have no idea how, I could tell this wasn't the same babyish crying as before. Kelly—bless her—took him in her arms and just held on while he sobbed. Norm managed to get out the words "It's bad." Kelly didn't seem surprised by that at all, and said, "I know. That's what I've been trying to tell you. Don't worry. We'll get through whatever it is. Together."

Well, that finished him. He broke down completely and started shaking all over. She eased him down onto the couch, holding him firmly the whole time. Truth is, it was probably me who was shaking. Crying? No. Shaking? Maybe. No way I was prepared for any of this! I'm actually wondering if maybe this therapy could be a good thing for Norm! But how can I possibly be dumb enough to think such a thing? Somehow I've got to get a grip. But at the moment, I simply don't know how! I think lurching out into the session was just about as hard on me as it was on Norm! But the opportunity was staring me in the face, and I simply could not refuse.

After a long time the shaking stopped, and Kelly asked if there was anything he could tell her about what happened. He could only say, "I don't know. I really don't. It was like a demon came out of me and snapped at Doc something awful. Somehow he wasn't scared at all, and talked back to it like he'd seen things like that before. Said he was glad it came out, and he thought it could help us. The main thing I remember is Doc saying I wasn't crazy. Boy, did I need to hear *that*!"

I could tell Norm waited a while to get up the courage, and then he asked her, "YOU don't think I'm crazy, do you?"

Kelly shook her head gently from side to side. "Not even a little bit. I just think there are a few problems that need to be worked on. Yes, they're serious problems, but it sounds to me like you've connected with someone who knows how to help. I can't tell you how glad I am about that!"

ENTRY 11:

Norm slept like a baby that night. I didn't force any dreams or any pain on him. I thought he deserved a break after what he'd been through. So now I have to wonder: is anything actually different? He hasn't had a night's sleep like that in a long time. Is that a good sign? Have I been wrong about Doc? Boy, do I not like this confusion! Anyway, the next session went like this:

NORM: "Well, I have some good news. Seems that Kelly is not going to give up on me, even if I'm demon-possessed. You can imagine what a relief that is to me."

Doc: "I can't tell you how glad I am to hear that. Support from someone who loves you is tremendously helpful in this work. Were you able to tell her what happened?"

"Just a bit, but she got the general idea. The whole thing leaves me with a thousand questions, like: Who was that character? Why is he so distrustful of you? And the main one: why did I almost black out when he was yelling at you? I mean, I was conscious the whole time. And believe me, I tried to stop it from happening. But IT was stronger than me. And I'll tell you—that was not a good feeling! Being that out of control is terrifying to me."

Doc: "I certainly understand that. I think in time you'll find that you can go along with it and derive some real benefit from it. As for your questions: for the first two, we'll have to let him— IT—provide those answers. For the last one, you have to realize he's connected with some events in your life that were extremely painful. There's a good chance some of those things made you black out either partly or completely. Now when he comes out, there's a tendency to do the same thing—black out partially. And there's another possibility: it may be that he comes out *when* you begin to black out, to help you in some way. Whatever it is, you'll get used to it, and over time you'll be wide awake the entire time, and much more in control of yourself. Believe me, I understand what a shock this is to your whole system right now."

"Boy, you got that right! Having gotten a good look at that freak makes me afraid of what other creeps might be lurking inside."

Doc: "Once again, I know these are just words, but I'm telling you there are no 'creeps' in there. They often seem frightening or ugly at first, but I meant what I said last session—you'll find them to be your friends in the long run."

But still, what if he's telling the truth? Man, this whole business is making me crazy. The very idea of trusting Doc is absurd. Or at least I always thought so. It's pretty obvious that he's different from Ted. But *how* different? And for how long? Is the axe just getting raised higher in the air, so it's more devastating when it falls? Almost in spite of myself, I decided to try another dream, but this time with the slight hope it might lead to getting rid of some of the pain. I'll probably hate myself for this. But like I said before, I can't quit.

ENTRY 12:

Next session, Norm reported it.

> NORM: "It went like this: I got caught in a hailstorm, and the stones were unusually big. Enough so the top of my head was badly bruised. I kept looking around for some cover, or for someone to help me, but nobody was paying any attention. Oddly, it seemed they weren't being struck by the stones like I was. Now what's that about?"

> DOC: "Do you remember in one of our early sessions feeling pain right on top of your head? Seems like it followed soon after reporting another dream. Is that right?"

> "Yeah, I think so. It was the first glimpse I ever got of the dungeon, and there was somebody crying. Do you think there's some kind of connection there?"

> DOC: "It's quite possible. And I think the fact there was nobody around to help you in this dream is probably also meaningful. Is that a familiar feeling for

you—being in pain and having nobody willing or able to help you?"

"I'll tell you what comes to mind right away is Aunt Sadie. She knew perfectly well all about Ted and what he did to me as a little guy, and sat by like a disinterested onlooker. I never could understand how she could do that. Seems like any decent person would have *had* to stop him from beating on a little kid. Occasionally she would say something real timid, but he paid no attention whatsoever. I can remember some dreams about beating her up! I know it was *him* I really wanted to go after, but I was so terrified I couldn't imagine it, even in my sleep!"

Doc: "A lot of times when men get drunk they do serious damage. You said that you recall some beatings from him. Is that right?"

"Yeah. Years ago, Maggie used to tell me about how bad it got, but I could never remember many of the details. All I know is I hated him like I never hated anybody else in my whole life. Later on, I had serious thoughts about how to kill him, but was too scared to ever carry them out. He's dead now, and so is Aunt Sadie, and the world's a lot better place for it."

33

Doc nodded in agreement. "It seems to me if you hated him that much, the beatings must have been awfully bad. Even if you don't remember much about them."

"Yeah, I've wondered about that. Just thinking about him right now makes my blood boil! One other thing: I've often wondered why he didn't beat Maggie like he did me. I mean, I'm grateful as I can be for that. But it just puzzles me. And yet, despite that, she turns out to be about half crazy anyway! It just doesn't add up."

Doc: "It's really a shame she won't talk about it. I'm betting that *something* happened back there to get her to where she is. Were there many times that she was alone with Ted?"

"I know what you're thinking. No. Not that I know of. Wait a minute . . . it's starting again . . . the pain. (Grabs the top of his head.) OW! . . . Doc, I've got to get out of here! This is killing me!"

Norm practically ran straight out the door, holding his head the whole time. And yeah, that was me making it happen. Seemed like the ideal time. But sometimes I wonder if I still really care about him, or if part of me *wants* to hurt him. He's rejected me so many times over the years, I wonder if I've come to just resent him more than anything. I've almost gotten to the point where it's actually painful to think about rejoining him. It's been so long, and there is so much that's happened. I guess part of me is close to giving up. But regardless of all that, I did what I did. Now I just have to wait it out and see what happens to him.

ENTRY 13:

When Norm got home, obviously in a lot of pain, Kelly tried to help him! She hasn't always done that. Lots of times she is so mad at him she doesn't seem to care if he's hurting or not. Thinks it's just another one of his games or something. But this time she got him some aspirin and some ice for his head. He was really grateful, and managed to tell her so. She looked at him funny, like she was trying to see if he was serious. I guess she gets just as tired as I do of being played for the fool.

ENTRY 14:

Next session, Doc started by asking Norm how he was feeling about the possibility of having what he called "Ego States" or "Parts" inside him. Norm said he still much preferred to think of them as *moods*. Doc said, "I can easily understand your reluctance. 'Parts' seem much closer to Multiple Personality Disorder, and in a way they are close. But they're not as hard to deal with, and they often have a lot to offer in the therapy process."

NORM: "You mean I'm going to get healed by internal demons?"

DOC: "I promise you they're not demons. I know the one who snarled at me a couple sessions ago was pretty scary for you. But I'll bet you a nickel he's just trying to defend you. In fact, for now I'm inclined to refer to him as a 'protector.'"

"But who the devil is he trying to 'protect' me from?"

DOC: "Quite possibly from me, for one thing. If you remember back to your talk with Maggie, it seemed clear there were some painful events she had forgotten about completely. You also wondered if maybe there were some things *you* had forgotten. If that's true, and the pain is stuck somewhere in your head and your body, it's going to try to work its way out into the open, bringing the pain with it. You, Norm, can't possibly *want* that to happen."

"This whole thing sounds like a bad movie so far. But what are you getting at, anyway?"

Doc: "I think we've met one of the Parts—the one I'm calling the protector. It's possible he's the one who brought you some of your dreams. Especially the one about me in the white coat, pretending to help you but then abandoning you when you really needed me."

Well, that was just too much. He was getting way too smart and *way too close*! Part of me was getting really excited with the idea that Doc might be able to actually help us. But then I saw that axe way up there in the air. All the old fears flared up inside me, and I made Norm holler out loud at Doc: "Leave me alone! I can't do this!"

Of course that sent him streaking right out the door. I was afraid I'd made a terrible mistake, but it was a done deal. I knew what was going to happen when Norm got home. Sure enough, he headed straight for the fridge. Luckily, Kelly wasn't home at the time. But the boys were, and Norm, still confused and about half crazy, lit into them right off. Made no sense what he was hollering about. He didn't care. Just had to spit out all that venom. After he calmed down a bit, Jake, his younger son, asked him a question: "So I guess the therapy is a waste of time, huh?" This made Norm even madder. "How the hell do you know about the therapy, boy?" he yelled at him. Jake just turned around and ran to his room, crying.

When Kelly got home soon after, he asked her, angrily, "How did Jake know I was in therapy?"

"I had to tell the boys," Kelly responded. "They were talking about going to live with some of their friends to get away from you. I had to try to stop that."

Norm was speechless. I guess he had no idea things were that bad. He just stood there motionless for a long time. Then he sat down, put his head in his hands and started crying. I could feel somebody making their way to the front, to pull their usual crap to sweeten everything up. But a very unusual thing happened. Norm must have felt it coming too, and said, "NO! Not you again! It's not that goddam easy!"

Well, this really scared Kelly. She of course had no idea about whoever this was. She assumed he was yelling at *her*! She said, "Now wait just a minute! I never said anything was easy about this!"

Norm just shook his head back and forth, saying, "No. No. It's not you. It's some damn demon." I heard Kelly take in a sharp breath, like she'd been hit in the stomach. Norm heard it too, and said, "No, I didn't mean that. It's just that it *feels* like a demon. It's that part of me that cries and begs and kisses butt, but then allows it to happen again and again. I felt it coming on, and knew how it was all going to play out, and I could NOT do it again! That's all I know."

Once again, Kelly surprised me, in a good way. For not knowing much of anything about what had been happening in the therapy, she seemed to understand well enough to not get mad at him. She asked him calmly, "Is this something I need to know about?"

Norm took several deep breaths. Finally he said, "I guess so. I just wish *I* knew about it! Doc thinks my 'moods' are something more than that. He calls them 'Parts' or 'Ego States.' Says they hold bad stuff from childhood I've made myself forget, and they're trying to bring it back. For some crazy reason, he thinks that would be a GOOD thing!"

Kelly took a long, deep breath and said, "Boy, am I glad to hear that! Somebody finally gets what I've been trying to tell you all along. Oops. I'm sorry. I don't think you need any 'told-ya-sos' right now."

"No. Definitely not. But it does make me think if you *and* Doc see it that way, I'd better

ALAN MARSHALL, PH.D.

pay attention. It's so hard for me to believe, but maybe you both want to help."

At that, he started crying all over again. But it was different this time too! It didn't sound like a baby. Sounded more like a real grown-up. Holy cow! Don't tell me something is changing. Nah, no way. I gotta stop thinking stuff like that. I'm not stupid enough to fall for that nonsense.

ENTRY 15:

Next session, Norm told Doc about what happened.

NORM: "To tell the truth, when I walked out last time, I had no intention of coming back. But being able to sense that babyish part coming out and being able to actually stop it gave me serious hope. So I guess you're right about these 'Parts' or whatever you call them. They *are* in there, and they do come out and control me part of the time. But how in heaven's name did they *get* there, and how do we get rid of them?"

DOC: "Whoa, wait a minute. Before long, you'll understand how they got there. But as for getting rid of them, I'm not sure you'll need to, or even want to, in

40

the long run. In the meantime, however, I think we might need to establish direct contact with them. Do you feel up to trying that?"

"I guess I really don't have any choice. All I can say is I'll try not to run out on you again."

Doc: "Please don't worry about that, just so you come back when you're ready. Would you mind closing your eyes?" He did, and Doc proceeded to say: "I'm pretty sure you've heard every word that's been said, so you know I think of you as a 'protector.' But at the same time, I also imagine you have needed to guard against Norm becoming too involved in this process. Is that true?"

No words came out of me, just a grunt, which Norm reported to Doc.

Doc said, "I'll take that as more or less a 'yes.'

Then a softer grunt.

Doc: "Okay, I'd like to ask you a couple of questions. First, are you aware of anyone else in there?"

Norm said he thought he heard the word "maybe."

"Second, even though you don't know who they are, do you know anything about how they influence Norm?"

I wasn't about to answer Doc directly, but I reminded Norm again of the incident where he was able to stop whoever it was doing the babyish crying, and he answered instead.

"It's still so hard for me to believe this stuff, but I recall saying 'not you again' as though I were talking to another person. What made me say that? I've been playing out this routine most of my life—why do I suddenly think 'somebody else' is involved?"

Doc: "I think part of the reason it might be different now is that we're talking out loud about all this, and you're more in touch with the possibility that 'they' are in there. How do you think this Part—if that's what it is—influences your daily life?"

"As far as I know, he stays out of the picture mostly, and just shows up when I've done something wrong—or at least believe that I have. As much as I'm disgusted by 'him,' I'll have to say he sounds real sincere. Or at least he used to, until I unmasked him. So I guess, before Kelly, a lot of people would have felt sorry for me and let me off the hook for whatever I'd done wrong."

DOC: "Yeah—little children who are sobbing are hard to come down on. Would you mind if I ask him just one more question?"

"Why not? It can't get any nuttier than it already is."

DOC: "I'm asking the protector now—is there any way to tell roughly about the age of the babyish one?"

I showed Norm the number four, sort of wiggly to let him know I wasn't sure about it, and he told Doc.

DOC: "Thanks again. Norm, this might not make any sense to you right now, but direct contact like this can be very difficult and tiring for Parts. I'd suggest we stop this for now, and give him—and you—a break."

Another grunt.

Doc went on, "I want to say one more thing to him, though: I think things are a little better for Norm now that you've come out more. His headaches seem to be gradually getting a little better, and I think Kelly is more able to tolerate the bad times knowing he—and you—are working as hard as you can on them. I'm very grateful to you for the help. But I need to say something to adult Norm." Doc pauses. "Norm, we're at a crucial point here, and it will help a lot if you can move toward making a difficult change. It can't happen suddenly, but I'd like you to give it some thought."

"Sure sounds ominous. Go ahead—I can stand it."

Doc seemed to measure his words very carefully. "It's about the pain. I know you hate it and are sick and tired of it. And I think you're beginning to understand that the Parts are causing a lot of it."

"Yeah, and you persist in calling them my 'friends' despite that. So what the devil are you getting at?"

Doc looked at Norm squarely and said, "Imagine for a moment that you live in a house with a rattlesnake. If you make yourself forget about it, it can kill you. But what if a Part of you reminds you about it often by pinching you or somehow causing sharp pain so that you'd never forget it completely—wouldn't your chances of surviving be a lot greater?"

"Yeah, but wouldn't it make me scared and nervous a lot of the time?"

Doc: "For right now, yes. But it seems to me better than being dead. And in my experience, getting through the rest of the pain can make for some serious improvement in your daily life, including reduction of that same fear and nervousness."

"But what does all that have to do with the pain on the top of my head?"

Doc responded, "We don't know yet. But since it came right on the heels of telling me a dream, I'll bet you a nickel it's connected to some childhood trauma. The kind of pain the Parts inflict is almost always directly connected with the original trauma, and it can take any form necessary: physical pain, mental suffering and even sickness."

"I still don't get it. Okay, let's suppose he's my friend and is trying to warn me or remind me about something. If it's something I've already experienced, what's the point of forcing me to go through it all over again?"

Doc seemed relieved, shook his head up and down and said, "That's a very good question. The point is that you only went through *part* of it—the part you could tolerate. But there's more: the part you did *not* experience. I'll wager there's somebody inside who took that on for you, and is trying very hard to bring it back to you. Believe me, I know how strange this sounds. But I'd like you to think about it during the week, and let's take it up again next time . . ."

Well, that knocked me sideways! How the devil does Doc know about this stuff? It almost sounds like he's trying to *help* me come out! But that's just impossible. Nobody has ever come close to doing that, and I'm not about to be sucked into believing he will either. He's only seen a small part of the pain I carry. Once he gets an inkling of how bad it is, he'll turn tail and run along with Norm. I know it. I'm no fool.

ENTRY 16:

When Norm got home from the session, Jake and Paul were playing hackysack in the front yard. As Norm was getting out of the car, Paul hollered at him, "Hey Pop, let's see whatcha got!" and fired a shot right into Norm's midriff. Since the ball was very soft, there was no damage. But as soon as he collected himself, Norm grabbed the ball and made a vigorous kick at it. He was not in good form, however, and fell flat on the ground. They could tell it was only his pride that was injured, and it got the boys to hooting something awful. Jake cried out, "What about all that soccer you played in college?" Norm brushed himself off and countered, "I told you that was intramural, not the real thing." Then he grabbed the ball again and tried another kick. Same result! That finished the boys. They were laughing so hard that it was contagious, and soon the three of them were rolling in the grass with delight, and loving every second of it. When Kelly called them to supper, Jake—breathlessly—said, "In a minute. Dad's teaching us the finer points of hackysack!"

At supper, Kelly said she had seen what happened and wished she had time to join in! She also noted that she had not seen Norm have that much fun in many years. I could tell she loved the whole business, especially seeing Norm's playfulness.

Early in the next session, Norm told Doc about it. Doc asked if it was true—that he hardly ever did anything so silly and fun. Norm said he had not done it in a long time, but it reminded him of being with his real parents. There was plenty of joy and fun then, even if only for a short time. Living with Ted's torture seemed to beat it out of him, and it was very hard to recapture. But the hackysack game seemed to bring it a little closer. At least for a little while.

DOC: "I don't mean to get all clinical on you here, but I wonder if there was one of your Parts involved. Possibly one who has preserved those memories of the good times. I'm also thinking of the crying you've described as 'babyish.' Most young children who can cry can also enjoy themselves thoroughly if given the opportunity."

NORM: "So I guess you're wanting to ask inside if there's a Part like that, right?"

DOC: "Only if you're okay with it. If there really is such a Part, and if it's anything like I think it might be, it's possible it could add some very good things to your life. I don't mean to deny there would be pain also. I think you're learned to just expect that."

"Yes, yes, there's always the pain. Dammit. All right, my eyes are closed."

48

After several minutes of quiet, Doc spoke.

"If you're in there, I imagine you've heard everything we've said. Is it possible for you to show Norm anything about yourself . . . or about what you remember? It can be in any form you choose."

Norm waited and waited, and was about to give up. Then he saw something: an image of a bear—a very fuzzy bear, like a child's doll. He told Doc about it and described it as he saw it—very fuzzy. He of course thought it was ridiculous and a waste of time and told Doc so.

But Doc asked: "I'm asking the Part now, is that true? Is this a waste of time?"

To my amazement, Norm shook his head no!

Norm opened his eyes and said, "Sorry to disappoint you. There just wasn't anything but that silly bear."

Doc: "You mean the fuzzy one?"

Norm said, "Yeah, why?"

Doc: "Did you know you shook your head no at some point? Namely, when I asked the Part if this was a waste of

49

time? It may not have been you who did it. It's quite possible the Part did it for you."

This made Norm really angry and he snapped, "You're making this up."

Doc: "No, I don't do that. Especially something important like this. I'm not trying to force this down your throat, but I want to suggest something to the Part. Is it okay with you if we call you 'Fuzzy'?"

Norm shook his head up and down excitedly! Than he grabbed the seat of the couch with both hands as though he was holding on for dear life. "Stop it! Stop it!" he said.

Doc said sheepishly, "I'm sorry. Sometimes I get a little out of control myself. Take a minute to get your bearings."

Norm got up and walked around the room several times. He said, "Yeah, I don't want you to do that again. Not unless I say okay. That was just too way out there. I feel very unsteady right now."

Doc: "I really do apologize. I'll try very hard to not do that again."

"Okay, but here's the strangest thing of all: I'm remembering it now; the second time, when I nodded my head up and down, I felt excited—like a little kid! Almost exactly like when I was rolling around in the grass." Finally he stopped circling the room, and sat down heavily. "So I guess there's more than one demon, huh? And before you correct me about that word again, I'm telling you I don't like this at all. If my head is going to shake yes or no, *I'm* the one who's going to do it, okay? These damn demon Parts can just keep their hands off me!"

Doc knew to keep his mouth shut for some time. Norm just kept fidgeting and stewing, angrily. He finally said, "You know the thing that bothers me the most about this? No? Well, I'll tell you: while this was all going on, I felt like I was trying to get back to my parents. Trying to feel that way again. I thought it was going to kill me. To feel that good. Almost like it was so close I could taste it. And then to come back to this room, and my real life, was just about unbearable."

I could tell Doc was dying to say something, but kept it to himself. I knew Norm's time was up, but Doc seemed determined to give him a little extra. Finally, Norm got up to leave, took a deep breath, and said, "I know I have

51

a lot to think about." He seemed to gather himself at the door, winked back at Doc and said, "Maybe I'll go play some hackysack." They both smiled.

Well, maybe *they* felt better, but I was even more confused. It was clear to me that somebody else made Norm do those things, like Doc said. But WHO? They're calling him "Fuzzy," but who the devil *is* that? I've been stuck in this danged prison for a long, long time and never heard anything from anybody else—ever. So who is this, and why are they choosing right now to come out? Man, everything seems out of control, bad. I don't see how this can possibly be a good thing.

ENTRY 17:

Next session:

> Norm started out by saying, "It didn't occur to me until later last week what I had said to Kelly when she saw me rolling in the yard with the boys. I said I had felt like that with my parents. Back in the good days. I'm amazed at how hard this is. You'd think I'd be delighted to feel anything like that, but it seems positively dangerous to me. Like if somebody promises you something that

would make you the happiest person in the world, but you know they're tricking you and you're going to be crushed."

Finally Doc said what I knew he'd been wanting to say last time: "Maybe it's not a trick."

"Yeah, that line went through my head too. I guess I'm just too old and too jaded to even be able to imagine such a possibility. It's way too painful."

I could feel that Doc resigned himself, and he said, "At any rate, we seem to be making some progress in other areas. Do you feel ready to continue?"

"To tell the truth, not right now. Can I call you when I'm ready?" Doc said sure, and Norm walked out the door like he weighed five tons.

ENTRY 18:

Something about what happened made Norm want to go see his sister. When he called, he was shocked to hear that he'd have to visit her in the hospital! She looked awful. Her eyes were sunk in, she had no color at all, and looked like she weighed half of what a normal person would—almost like a skeleton. Norm said, "What in the world is going on? Are you not eating anything that they give you?"

Maggie just shook her head very slowly, like it hurt to move any body part.

Norm sat down and said, "I'm sorry. I didn't mean to holler at you."

She said, "It's okay. Everybody treats me that way. Nobody understands."

"Understands what?"

"How I feel. They're always preaching at me about eating. Nobody seems to get it that I *can't* eat, because it makes me fat. Would you please talk to them about that?"

Norm could feel the uselessness of arguing with her. He'd tried that before, and it just drove a big wedge between them. He got up from his chair and said, "I'll be right back. I need to ask the nurse something."

What he asked the nurse was whether or not his sister was dying. She said, "It's possible. We've seen people like this before, and when they get this thin and this weak they sometimes don't make it. I'm very sorry to tell you that."

He went back to Maggie's room and said if she didn't feel like talking, not to do it. But he had some questions she might be able to help with. She said she'd try. First, though, he couldn't resist telling her about the delightful hackysack game with his sons. Anything to try to perk her up. Maggie tried hard to smile and almost did it. Norm could see what an effort it was for her and put his hand up to stop her. She did manage to whisper "I'm so glad."

He knew she meant it. Then he began the questions. "Maggie, I know you told me before that you don't remember much of anything about our life with Ted and Sadie. But, to tell you the truth, I'm having some problems, and have gotten into therapy, and I thought you might be able to fill in a couple of blanks. Are you strong enough to try?"

She nodded her head, wearily.

"Okay, now, we can quit anytime it's too much. I remember you told me years ago that you felt sorry for Ted. I couldn't imagine your saying it, and it confused me no end. Can you say anything about that?"

Maggie took several deep breaths, each one appearing to be painful. "I did, though. I know he hurt me, too, but he could be really nice sometimes. And often he would promise to stop hitting *you* if I would do . . . stuff with him."

Norm stared at her. "Well, I can tell you he usually broke his promise. But what do you mean by 'stuff'?"

Maggie didn't say a word for a great long time, like she was weighing in her mind if it should stay a secret, like she had kept it these many years. But then she burst out, "You know! Boy-girl stuff. I tried to tell you about it when we were younger, but you just didn't understand, so I gave it up. Norm, I'm getting worn out . . ."

"I know," Norm said. "It helps a little to know he could be nice to you sometimes. I didn't know he could do that with *anyone*! I can see you need to sleep, but do you mind if I just stay here a few minutes, just to be with you?"

Maggie, tearfully: "Of course not. Bye for now . . ."

There was no sound but slow breathing for a long time, and eventually Norm got up to leave. On the way out the door, he noticed Maggie humming something so softly he could barely hear it. He got down next to her and could make it out. It was a hymn they used to sing together—"The Old Rugged Cross." After a few more seconds, it stopped. Norm just made it to the safety of his car before he burst out crying. I don't know if it was the hymn or learning about what Ted did to his sis, but he cried for a very long time.

ENTRY 19:

Norm set up another session and told Doc about the visit.

"She really looked awful. I hated doing it, but I had to ask her a few questions.

She was so weak, I only managed one, but her answer shocked me terribly. I'm sure you remember asking if she and Ted were ever alone. Of course I knew what you were thinking, and you were dead right. And apparently he treated her a lot better than me, so she actually says she felt *sorry* for him!! How can you possibly feel 'sorry' for someone who is molesting you? How can she not hate him just as much as I do, or more?"

Doc: "I know what you mean. When I first started hearing about it, I thought the people—the victims— were plain crazy. And don't think for a minute that it's true for all of them. Some perpetrators are horrible beasts, and some are not, and everything in between. As far as I can tell, Ted was a beast to you, and not nearly the same to your sister. He still would go to jail for it today, regardless of how he treated her otherwise. Believe me, I know how hard it is to grasp all this."

"You got *that* right, buddy! And one other thing—if he wasn't totally awful to her, how in the world did she get so hopelessly screwed up?"

Doc: "And there's the rub. No matter how kind or gentle he may have been with her in other ways, the damage was still done. She still had to feel betrayed, and a thousand other things that would have confused her no end. And just the fact she had to keep it all secret, which I'm sure he made her do, caused it to be way worse. I still say he deserved prison time, at the very least."

"I have to tell you something I'm ashamed to admit: I think I knew it all along. Maybe it came from her telling me a little bit even when I didn't understand, or maybe I just knew it myself. I'm not sure. But I *am* ashamed I didn't pursue it, or do anything to try and stop it. I wonder if her life would be different now if . . ."

Doc: "Whoa there, now. Remember what your *own* life was like back then. You were just a little kid, terrified and hated by a huge man who beat you badly and often. What could you have done to him that wouldn't have gotten you beaten senseless, or killed. What good could it have possibly accomplished?"

"I know you're right. But seeing her lying there, getting ready to die . . . the whole thing is just plain sickening." He couldn't speak for some time. He finally said softly, "That reminds me, there was one other thing. When I was leaving and she was on the verge of sleep, she started humming this hymn, 'The Old Rugged Cross.' Do you know it?"

Doc: "Oh, sure. Just about anyone who has ever been to church knows it, I think. But it sounds like it meant something special to you. Is that true?"

"All I know is it gave me a very strange feeling. That night I couldn't go to sleep, listening back to it. And now that I think of it, she was right on the edge of sleep herself, and I couldn't figure out how she was humming! Could she have been doing it in her sleep?"

Doc: "That's possible. It's also possible she was in a sort of pre-sleep trance, and had dissociated from her customary adult self."

"What's that—'dissociation'?"

Doc: "It's just a word for something you already know about—when you get 'dizzy' from too much physical or psychological pain and somebody else inside takes over partly, for a while. From what you've told me about her history, it's very likely she would have some internal Parts just like you do."

"Man, this makes me even sadder she never got any help. I want to go visit

59

her again soon. It raises some more questions I'd like to ask her."

ENTRY 20:

A few days later, he was at the hospital again, and Maggie seemed a tiny bit better. Norm asked if that were true, and Maggie said, "Yeah, they're tube-feeding me now. I hate it. Still makes me gain weight. I guess they'll never understand how disgusting that is to me. Anyway, what did you want to know?"

Norm hesitated some, then spoke quietly. "When I was leaving last time, it seemed like you had already gone to sleep, and yet you were humming that hymn we used to sing together—'The Old Rugged Cross.' Do you remember doing that?"

Maggie shifted in the bed. "No, I think you imagined it. I haven't sung that or hummed it in years."

Norm found it hard to believe. "Really?" he said. "You don't remember doing it?"

"I told you no." Maggie was clearly irritated. "Why do you find that strange?"

Norm seemed to sense that he should quit the subject and said, "I'm not sure, but it doesn't matter. Just seemed a little odd. I do have one other question: do you remember the old barn out back at Ted's place?"

Maggie turned her head away, and took a sharp breath. "Yes, but that's not something I can talk about. You'll have to take that up with your doctor friend. I think it's time for you to leave."

I could tell Norm was hurt. But more than that, he was puzzled. He slept poorly the next few nights and couldn't get the hymn out of his head.

ENTRY 21:

Norm told Doc about it at the next session.

> "I'm sure she remembered something about the barn—something really bad. But she couldn't tell me. What do you suppose that's about?"

> Doc: "Remember my saying that even if Ted wasn't terrible to her, she would still have serious damage from the molestation? That may be the part she doesn't want to think about, or talk about. Sounds to me like she's going to take some of her secrets to the grave."

> "Speaking of the grave, she actually sounded farther away from it this time. She said they're tube-feeding her, and although she hates it, she seems a little stronger, thank God."

They talked about other stuff the rest of the session, but Norm soon regretted what he said. The hospital called that evening to say that Maggie had died! The nurse said it was very strange, because they had all seen her getting better, or so they thought. Norm demanded to know if there was anything else, and the nurse reluctantly told him Maggie had pulled all her tubes out, not just the feeding tube. "But," she said, "that should not have ended her life. It almost seemed like she just didn't want to live anymore, period. We've seen that happen before, but it always seems very strange, medically speaking."

Norm thanked her for the information and hung up. Then *he* wanted to die. He felt sure he had killed Maggie. Too many questions. Too much upset. Dragging her through things she couldn't stand to remember. How could he have done it? He loved her as much as he ever loved anyone. And now she was gone because of him. He wanted to dig a grave, and crawl into it himself.

He called and left a message for Doc, telling about Maggie, saying he'd get back with him later. But months went by, and there was no getting back later. He felt like he was drowning, and didn't want to take anyone else down with him. Kelly of course tried her best to help, but was unsuccessful. It seemed he was doomed. Kelly kept saying he was overreacting, which didn't help at all. She insisted there was no possible way he could have known what Maggie would do, and that she would probably have done it eventually anyway.

It all fell on deaf ears. He drank way more than usual and didn't go to work half the time. Finally, Kelly gave him a choice: either he go back and talk with Doc about it or she was leaving him. He said go ahead, he didn't care. She was gone by the next day, and the boys were with her.

I was at a loss myself. I had never seen him react like this to anything, no matter how bad. After a while, I couldn't stand it anymore, and forced a dream on him. In it, Maggie appeared in a beam of light, telling him she felt better now than she ever had in real life, and didn't blame him at all for the questions. She also said he should get back to Doc, because there were things about all this he didn't understand. Now, I admit this was all pretty far-fetched on my part, but I had to do *something*. And besides, I did honestly think something was wrong about all the guilt. I had no idea what it was, but I could feel it. Finally, he called Doc.

ENTRY 22:

Next session:

Doc began: "I got your message, and I'm terribly sorry to hear about Maggie. How've you been doing in the meantime?"

NORM: "Awful. Doc, it was my fault, her dying. I never told the nurse, but I got all worked up asking her questions she couldn't stand to answer. They were obviously too painful. But did that stop me? Hell, no! So I ended my sister's life. Kelly just doesn't get it. Not at all. I imagine you probably won't either."

DOC: "I can't say I do, yet. But I know you're not crazy, and there has to be something real behind this. Can you tell me anything more about it?"

Norm squirmed around in his chair for a long time, and finally said, "There's just one thing. We had been talking about the barn, and that's when she turned away. But I had also asked her about humming the hymn, and she denied knowing she did it. Something about the two things together is driving me crazy. I'm not sleeping at all, and when I do it's usually nightmares."

Doc: "Well, if there is more to it than we now know, somebody inside may have some of the answers. Do you feel like taking a look?"

For some reason, Norm teared up at the thought, but said he'd close his eyes. When Doc asked if there was anybody inside who could help, I knew I was at a loss. I had no clue. But then the tearing became outright sobbing, and pretty soon a little voice said out loud, "Yeah, maybe I can." Doc said he was really glad to hear from him, but added, "Remember—not too fast." At that, the voice retreated farther inside, but so Norm could still hear it. For some reason, I could too! "It's about the barn," it said. "Do you remember the stacks of hay?" Norm gagged, and headed for the bathroom. When he got back, he was wide awake, and the voice was gone.

It was almost the end of the session before Norm could tell about it.

Doc said he had heard the voice at first, and it sounded to him like a very young boy—kind of like one who had spoken briefly in an earlier session—the one they called "Fuzzy."

Norm: "I know. It sounded like that to me also, even when it stopped talking

65

out loud. He mentioned the stacks of hay in the barn, and it knocked me for a loop. I know I need to work on that. Maybe next time . . ."

Later that week, in the middle of the night, Norm awoke with a start. He sat bolt upright, and said, "Who's there?" He couldn't see much and got up and looked around, but saw nothing. Then he said, "I guess it's you. Maybe that means it's time. All right, I'm going back to the barn . . . with you . . ."

I don't know what happened after that, except for a lot of twisting and moaning, but I know within a half hour he was sleeping soundly.

ENTRY 23:

He told Doc about it, so I finally got filled in along with him.

"I could feel him there—the little guy— 'Fuzzy.' It made me remember a little bear I had that Dad gave me. That's what I called him. I could always tell him everything—the bear, I mean. Now it's his turn. He showed me the barn in great detail, things I had forgotten about long ago, even the smell of the hay. Then he told me to go inside, to where the hay was stacked. That was all I could do, and he disappeared. When I woke up, the bed sheets were all in a tangle, and soaking wet from sweat! I guess that *was* enough!"

Doc: "You did fine. That's a lot to remember at one sitting. Fuzzy, I'm glad you could help out. I have a hunch there's more to all this, but am sure glad we have your memory to count on. Norm, has this changed your feelings at all about Maggie?"

"Not really. I do have an odd sense that this is leading somewhere, even though I don't yet have any idea where. But it does feel good to hear from Fuzzy. I'd swear he sounds a lot like me at a young age. Is that possible?"

Doc: "Sure is. From the little bit I've heard, he sounds delightful. But we also can't forget about the pain he's carrying."

"Yeah, I know. But in the meantime, he reminds me so much of my parents, and the good years, it's comforting to hear from him."

The whole thing kind of irritated me. I mean, what's to get all giddy about? So sweet little Fuzzy remembers stuff—big deal. And so Norm feels a little better knowing he's around—big deal again. His wife and kids are still gone, and he's barely holding onto his job. Like I said before, I'm no fool. This means nothing to me. The axe is still hanging up there, just waiting. And I'm still completely alone.

I'll admit one thing, though. This kid and I seem to have something in common. We both try to get things through to Norm that he's forgotten about, and it always seems to involve pain. So we may be a bit alike. But we're way different in other ways. He's a silly little dude, playing around in the grass with other kids, and crying at a moment's notice. But I guess the bottom line is that he remembers things I don't, and maybe that can help Norm in the long run. But was there a time when he was inside Norm like I was? Is he just as alone as I am? I swear this is making me completely crazy. I hate the going back and forth from feeling hopeful to being sure the whole thing is one big trap, like it was fifty other times. I'll just have to see what develops.

ENTRY 24:

A couple of weeks went by fairly quietly, then one day there was a big surprise: Kelly and the boys came home! It wasn't the most joyous reunion ever, though. She just figured Jake and Paul should be with their father and decided to join them. She had not heard about Maggie and was truly sorry. Norm didn't go on much about it, expecting to be accused again of overreacting. But I could tell how glad he was to see Kelly. To my surprise, he told her some about Fuzzy! That was something that interested Kelly a whole bunch. She asked a lot of questions, and I thought she was glad they seemed to be making some progress. Norm told Doc about it next time.

Doc said: "I'm really glad to hear they're back. I hope it can stay that way. She sure seems to care a lot for you."

"I know. I'm actually a pretty lucky guy."

Doc: "Have you heard anything more from inside?"

"Just when Kelly first got back. I could feel myself get really excited, and wanted to hug her and hang on to her forever. That's not like the regular me."

Doc: "Did you do it?"

"No, but to tell the truth, I really wanted to. She just didn't seem nearly as excited to be back as I was to have her. I didn't want to put myself out there and get rejected again."

Of course I thought, *Now you're catching on. Don't get your hopes up. You'll just get smashed.* But then Norm said, "She did say one thing, though—she thought we were making headway in this work and was very glad to hear it."

So he got sucked in part of the way. I don't know if he'll ever learn. What's he going to do if he gets as stupid as ol' Fuzzy? I don't think I want to be any part of that. It may be time for a dream. Something to steady things down for a while.

ENTRY 25:

Norm reported it next time:

"In the dream, some man was playing a game in some sort of tournament, and he was doing well. Then, out of nowhere, they changed the rules, and he was humiliated. Not only did he lose, but he was laughed at by all the other players. Not a very fun game!"

Doc: "What does that remind you of?"

"Actually, nothing. I mean, my life is going a little better right now, so you could say I'm 'winning' in some ways. But why would the rules get changed, and me get humiliated?"

Doc: "You know I don't like trying to interpret your dreams for you, but I can't help thinking of Fuzzy. He's a little kid, and little kids have lots of fun, and they can readily forget about their pain for a time in order to enjoy the moment. But when you think about that as an adult, is having that much fun not a little scary?"

"You mean because they may be setting me up for later disappointment? You don't have to tell me about that. Not many people are more cynical than I am. But so what if that's true of Fuzzy? Isn't it just part of his nature?"

Doc: "Yes, I think it might be. But it's very likely there would be a counterbalancing Part inside you also— one who tries to protect you from just that sort of disappointment. Does that make any sense to you?"

"I suppose. But what are you getting at?"

"Misunderstanding," said Doc. "It's an important thing for us to start working on. I'll bet you the various Parts inside you understand each other very poorly, if at all. And that creates conflict, and drains your energy and keeps you confused. You have to remember they came at different ages, and they have

71

different memories, so they're working in different realities. That's part of why it's so important for them to come out and tell about their individual experiences. Once each one hears what the others went through, it becomes clearer why they feel and act the way they do. Gradually, the conflict dissipates, and they can begin working more as a team, on your behalf."

"Sounds simple enough. Why didn't they figure this out themselves?"

Doc: "For one thing, they most likely didn't even know the others existed until you got into this work."

"But if they didn't know about each other, how could they get into conflict?"

Doc: "You're no dummy, are you! When they cause a person to behave in very different ways, there is inevitable conflict in day-to-day life. When they understand each other better, things go smoother. Does that make any sense to you?"

Well, whether Norm or Doc understood at all, I was a little bit excited by it! It made me think maybe Fuzzy wasn't so stupid after all. Maybe he just had different experiences than I did— ones that made him laugh and cry and do lots of things of things I can't. Much as I hate to admit it, that might make a whole lot of sense! Right at this moment it's giving me a crazy idea. What if, next time Fuzzy is around, I try to talk with him myself? Boy, it's wild to think a thought you've never thought before! But it might be worth a try.

ENTRY 26:

Doc surprised me again. Turns out he had been thinking almost the same thing I was, about me and Fuzzy meeting. He proposed the idea to Norm and got him to relax.

> Then Doc said, "I'm pretty sure both of you can hear me. I don't think you've ever met, but it might be a good thing for Norm if you did. I'm not sure I understand exactly how the dungeon is set up, but I believe you must be in different cells down there. Is it possible for one of you to speak to Norm, so that the other might be able to hear it?"

I could tell Norm was listening as hard as he could, and I said, "I guess I'm willing to hear from this other character, if he's really down here."

Norm told that to Doc, and then waited a while for Fuzzy to show up. He didn't exactly do that, but Norm said to Doc, "I'm not hearing anything directly from him, but when the other one spoke, I could feel a sort of chill go through me, like I was a bit excited. That may be all he can do for now."

Doc: "That's fine. I would like to ask the other one a question: is there a name you'd like to be called? We've decided to call the other one 'Fuzzy,' and it would be a little easier if we had a name for you also."

I told Norm that Ted used to call me "Brat," and I was used to it. So now I have an official name: Brat! I told Norm to ask Doc if, now that there were so many of us, Norm would have to pay group rates. Doc chuckled, and said he'd heard that one a few times already, but was glad to know I had a sense of humor.

A few nights later, I was awakened by a soft voice. It was Fuzzy! He said he was sorry he couldn't speak the other day, but he still has a hard time trusting Norm and Doc. I had no trouble agreeing with him on that! I asked him how old he was, and he said four. I told him I was eight, and he said, "Boy, you're about fifty times older than me!" Made me laugh, hearing four-year-old arithmetic.

Then he got real serious and said, "You know some about the hymn, don't you?" I said yes, and he continued, "Well, there's more to it. Some tough stuff." Made me think of Doc saying there's always pain, too. Then he told me about a dream he intended to take to Norm. It gave me the creeps for some reason I couldn't identify.

ENTRY 27:

Next session Norm began:

"I heard the hymn again, in this dream. It was so soft I could barely make it out, but it seemed to be coming from the barn. When I realized it was Maggie humming it, I awoke in a start. I laid there for a while afterward, trying to remember if I ever got really close to the barn. I'm not sure, but I think I got as close as the outside door. That's probably why I was able to hear her."

Doc: "Can you remember how you were feeling, either in the dream or afterward?"

"I seemed to get sicker and sicker as it went on, and even more so when I was awake. Finally I had to get up and walk around to shake it off. Kelly asked me what was wrong, but I couldn't tell her anything."

Doc: "Did Ted show up in the dream anywhere?"

"Uh-oh. That hurts! I mean my head. It's the aching again, right on top." Norm closed his eyes and covered his head with his hands. He stayed that way a long time, moaning. Then he said, very softly, "Now I know why he beat me on the top of my head: it left no scars! That bastard! Sometimes he would grind his knuckles in so hard it would tear out some of my hair. But not enough so anybody would notice. Said if I told anybody, he'd do the same to Maggie. Of course that shut me up for good. I really wish he weren't dead, so I could kill him again!"

On the way home, I realized something very odd: I felt different! I mean, not a *whole* bunch, but definitely some. Almost like I was a little lighter or something. Then, when Norm got home, he told Kelly the same thing: *he* felt a little different! I didn't know what to think. Why would that be? I knew I got rid of part of the pain, back to where it belonged. But why didn't that make him feel *worse* like it had so many other times? One thing I was sure of: it wouldn't last. No doubt about it. Nice to get a little relief, for both of us. But it would all come back. I was totally certain of it. I'm no fool.

Sure enough, a couple of nights later, somebody was mad at me. It was Fuzzy! He was louder than usual, complaining that I butted in on his dream. He said, "Sure, you got your two cents in, but what about me? You made him remember *your* pain, so I'm still stuck with all of mine!" I told him I had no idea where the dream was heading, and it just seemed like a good way to bring some things back to Norm. Then he started crying, and it made me feel sorry for him, something I didn't know I could feel. So I promised him next time I'd stay out of it. He said, "I have to admit, I noticed both of you felt a little better. I'm glad about that. I just hope he'll feel better after *I'm* done with him!"

Something about seeing him soften gave me some courage, and I asked him the thing I'd been afraid to ask all along: "Were you part of Norm at one time?" He said, "Yes, absolutely. And now I know you were too. I'm sure you've suffered just like I have being torn away from him for so many years. I'd almost given up hope of it really happening, but this work with Doc seems like it's headed in that direction. For myself, I'd be delighted to get *partway* back, even if not totally. The reason I say that is because there are some things I would have to bring back that I'm not sure he could stand. Things you don't know any more about than he does."

Well, I didn't like hearing that at all. For one thing, I hated the idea of him knowing stuff I didn't. And secondly, it pissed me off that he might be smarter than me. So I left him there. Went right to sleep. No way he could stop that.

ENTRY 28:

Next session Norm told Doc about feeling a little better, maybe a bit more optimistic for some reason he couldn't identify. Doc said he was very glad, and that there was not always a direct connection between events in therapy and changes in how a person feels.

> Doc: "It's something I have wondered about a lot, and understand very little. I know for myself, the changes would often take me by surprise. I'd only realize after the fact that I had reacted differently in a difficult situation, with less anxiety or whatever. I have this picture in my mind of a deep, dark recess in the mind where these things get worked out among the various Parts, and we only feel the effects later. Whatever it is, I'm grateful for it."

Norm then added, "I guess so. But the guilt is still with me. I had something happen the other day, right while I was supposed to be working. Just some images. There was this little doll, kind of like Fuzzy, and he was headed for the barn. That was it. It shook me up bad, though. I had to leave work early. Luckily, it was a slow day, and nobody noticed."

Doc: "That *is* unusual, to see something like that during work. Most times they wait until you're alone, or sleeping, or about to. Maybe he thinks this can't wait."

"I wondered the same thing. I can't believe I'm suggesting this, but maybe I should close my eyes and see if I can get more out of it." He did that, and allowed his breathing to slow way down. Nothing happened for a long time, and then finally he said, "I'm hearing it again—the hymn." Then he got quiet again. I lost interest and was about to go to sleep, when he said, "Oh no. No, no." After a long time, Doc asked what it was, and he said, "Fuzzy is changing into me. Now it's me—and Fuzzy—headed for the barn. And I can still hear the hymn. It's Maggie. She's humming it. Why is this making me feel sick? It's so bad I don't want to be there." Then his voice got real low, and he whispered, "I don't want to be there." Then he jerked upright, wide awake.

Doc and Norm were both real quiet for a very long time.

Finally, Norm said, "You know, don't you. You know what I did." At that, he turned away from Doc like he was ashamed of something.

DOC: "I guess maybe I do. Can you tell me about it?"

"No wonder I felt guilty about her dying. I killed her twice. Once in the hospital, and once . . ." He couldn't finish the sentence. Finally, Doc offered, "In the barn?"

Norm nodded his head, just one time. Then the tears poured out.

He sputtered, "How could I have left her? I may not have known exactly, but I knew something terrible was going on in there, and I DID NOT stop it. He did whatever he wanted with her, and I allowed it, and it killed her. What kind of . . ."

Doc offered him tissues, but Norm could not turn back toward him to get them. As he stumbled out the door, he just kept saying, "I'm sorry. I'm sorry."

ENTRY 29:

Norm was in a daze for several weeks. He stayed away from Doc and tried to forget what happened. Kelly seemed to sense that it was very bad, whatever it was. Finally she got him to talk about it. After he told her, she had no idea what to say. She just felt so sorry for him she couldn't stand it. And *she* felt guilty! Now she finally understood why he had been apologizing his whole life for things he didn't do, because of something he *couldn't* do! Something no child in the *world* could do. And she had gotten furious! If only there was some way to take it back. To take it *all* back. All she could do was hold him, and after a long time that seemed to help. He appreciated it more than he could tell her, but she seemed to know anyway.

After another week or so, he finally got up the courage to call Doc. By that time, it had become clearer to him what really happened. He had headed to the barn because he sensed his sister was in danger, and he desperately wanted to help. But when he heard the humming, it made him realize it was over, whatever it was they were doing. It made him very sick to his stomach, and he ran away as fast as he could go. And then— finally—the thought came: what else could he have done? He knew better than anyone what Ted would do if he went in there—just beat him half to death. And the truth is, like Doc had said, that would not have done anyone any good.

But, by God, he *tried*! He got as far as the door, which by itself probably endangered his life. Running away didn't mean he didn't love his sister. It meant what was done was done, and there was no point in dying because of it. He somehow knew he would never get over it completely, but at last he could give up feeling so much guilt about it. There was no need.

When he finally said it all out loud, Doc was both very sad and very pleased, I could tell. Sad because he knew what Norm had lived with all these years, and pleased that now there was a good chance things would be different somehow.

And they did seem to be. Norm was a little bit happier person. That was clear to Kelly, and she was glad. As were the boys. The headaches were not as frequent, and the apologizing slowed down. And Norm found more time to play hackysack with Jake and Paul, even if it was ridiculous-looking fun. So we all assumed it was over. At last!

Given some free time, I got to talking with Fuzzy more. I told him about how hard it had been for me to believe anything good could happen in the therapy, and he understood!

He said, "Well, of course! You came out at a time in Norm's life when he was miserable and bitter, so of course you were too. How could you not bring some of his feelings with you?" I didn't understand how a four-year-old could know such a thing, but just accepted it, gladly. He added, "It was different for me. I had just lost my—I mean our—real parents, but I still had a basic belief that things would get back to being better, like they were with them. So I was partly *glad* when he connected up with Doc. I've just always been hopeful. I never had as much pain to deal with as you did, so I didn't have to sleep nearly as often. But even then, I never knew you were around until you finally came all the way out. And I never knew about how you felt until recently. And like somebody said, the differences between you and me sure did make for plenty of misunderstandings!"

I didn't say a word.

"But there's one thing I think we both can agree on: we're a little closer to Norm than we were before the therapy. I don't know about you, but I know for me that's very encouraging. I'm still hoping as the years go by we can find a means to get all the way in."

Then he said one last thing that sent a chill through me: "Maybe we won't have to be so hard on him now. Let's see how he does with all this." I hated the sound of that word "maybe." I decided the first thing I needed was a little sleep. After that, like Fuzzy said, we'd "see how he does."

Chapter Two

ENTRY 1:

A lot of time has gone by—maybe four years. The boys are in college, and Norm and Kelly are still married and still have their jobs. Overall, they're doing well, but something is stirring. I can feel it. Norm has been edgy, like some little something is crawling underneath his skin. He's not snapping at Kelly, but she can sense something isn't right. After several weeks of hoping it would go away on its own, she suggested he give Doc a call. The first session back seemed like old times.

DOC: "I'm sure glad to hear things are going better, even if not perfectly. What's up?"

NORM: "I wish I knew. I can tell I'm off center. It's hard to concentrate at work, and I'm a little irritable with Kelly. She thought I ought to call you."

Doc: "So once again she's the instigator! Well, I'd say she got it right last time, so let's see what we can find. Have you been dreaming?"

"No, hardly at all. I can tell you where the trouble seems to be mostly, though: in my heart. I'm not worried about a stroke or anything, but something in there doesn't feel right. A lot of times just before I fall asleep, I'll notice it's beating unusually fast, enough so it worries me. I had an exam, and the usual tests, and they showed nothing wrong. In fact, one guy said I should live to be a hundred. So that's not it."

Doc hesitated some, and then asked: "Do you notice any other physical sensations that are unusual?"

"No, except I get a little teary sometimes for no apparent reason."

Doc: "Are you ever aware of what you're thinking about at such times?"

"It's not always, but sometimes I'll be thinking back to the times with my real parents. Silly stuff, like the games we played in the car, or in the bed when we'd wake them up in the morning. As soon as I say that, I realize I've stopped playing hackysack with my boys. That's not a good sign. When they're home from college, I notice them hanging around in the front yard sometimes when I get home, like it's an invitation to come have fun. The only one missing out is me."

Doc: "When that happens, are you aware of what you're feeling?"

"Yeah. Sad. Depressed, I guess. That's a new one for me. I never even thought of that word until right now. I always thought depressed people were just crybabies who needed to get over it. I suspect that will be a little different from now on."

Doc: "Yeah. I've often wondered if maybe we don't want to feel the pain they're going through, and so we deny it, or even make fun of it."

"Whatever it is, I'm now on the other end of it, and I don't like it. It hurts!"

Doc: "That's exactly what I mean. Who would want to feel that along with you?"

"Obviously, nobody. Except for Kelly. And even then it's not that she *wants to*, at all."

Doc: "So, bottom line, this is something you're basically alone with. Right?"

"You just hit a nerve, Doc. That word 'alone' got to me. Okay, you don't have to remind me what to do. I'll close my eyes and see what wonderful insight occurs to me. (Several minutes pass, and his breathing slows down.) So far it's just the same stuff. Happy times with Maggie and the parents. Lots and lots of them. (Opens his eyes.) I have a question here: okay, so those times really were that good, and I remember them mostly. What good does that do me? I mean, life with Kelly may not be quite like that—it can't ever be that carefree, with the feeling of being taken care of and secure all the time. Is that what's depressing me? Remembering and wanting something from childhood that just isn't possible in real life? Isn't that a waste of time?"

Doc: "I understand your question. And I'd say if that were all there is to it, yes, it would be a waste of time. But I wouldn't jump to that conclusion just yet. It's possible there are still some things going on in there we don't know about, and which might prove helpful. I'm more than willing to help you look, if you want."

Well, just like the first time, Norm wasn't all that hopeful, and I sure wasn't either. It was way too easy to remember how difficult the first go-round was, and I wasn't the least bit eager to do it again. What made it worse was I had no idea where we were headed. Before, I knew a lot about what was wrong, and wound up being able to help some eventually. But here I'm just lost. Funny I wrote that—I guess that's how Norm feels: lost. And alone.

ENTRY 2:

When Kelly asked how it went, Norm said he learned he might be depressed. She asked hopefully if there weren't some sort of medication that could help with that. Norm said they hadn't even discussed it, and for some reason it didn't seem to him to be the answer. Kelly tried to conceal her disappointment, but Norm sensed it. He said, "I think I'll try it with Doc for a while. If there's no improvement, maybe we'll go to an anti-depressant." Even though there was no open conflict, I could tell Norm was feeling even more alone now. He could easily understand why she would want a quicker cure, but he felt a bit abandoned by her. So he'd had one session, and the trouble had already started!

Made me remember right away why I had always been such a cynic!

That night I talked with Fuzzy about what happened. He claimed he hadn't been responsible for Norm feeling depressed, but that if it didn't go away on its own, he would probably have to bring something else back to Norm—something he had hoped to leave alone. I asked what it was, and he said, "It's what I told you about earlier, that I hoped I wouldn't have to bring up. It'll probably be best if you learn it along with Norm. You're not going to like it, but in the long run it should be helpful." Once again I wondered how this four-year-old could have ideas that complicated, but decided to try to accept maybe he was smarter than I gave him credit for.

ENTRY 3:

In the next session, Norm was asking Doc about the depression.

> "I'm a little worried this might be permanent," he said. "It's been going on now for over a month. Does that worry you?"

> "Not necessarily," Doc said. "This still qualifies as what we call 'acute' depression, which basically means it

would ordinarily go away on its own. But I have to say, knowing what I do about you, I'm not sure but what it's trying to tell you something. What has happened since our last session? Have you noticed anything unusual?"

"Well, it's unusual for me to lie awake thinking a lot about good times with my real parents. But that just strikes me as a way to get away from the sadness. And it doesn't work anyway. It starts out being fun, and winds up back here, being no fun at all."

Doc: "Have you thought about trying an anti-depressant?"

"Are you and Kelly in collusion again? That's what she suggested. And I can't blame her at all. She's been through some bad times with me, and would prefer not to do it again. What I think I want to do is see what you and I can find without medication. If nothing turns up, I'd certainly give it a try."

Doc agreed and said, "Sounds good to me. Let's go back to the thoughts about your parents for a minute. I know you told me they involve various games and such. Would you mind elaborating on that for me?"

"I can tell you what I was remembering last night. We used to travel a good ways to visit our grandparents, so of course there was a need for a way to occupy me and Maggie. It seemed like Mom always had a game up her sleeve to pass the time. Last night I remembered when she would point out some object way in the distance, and Maggie and I would each guess how far it was away. Then Dad would keep track on the odometer, and the winner would get a big hurrah. Maggie and I could get *very* competitive! But Mom had a way of making sure we each won some, so no blood was shed. But that's a good example about both parents: they always took time to make sure we had some fun, and neither kid was excluded." Then he lowered his head and got quiet.

Doc waited a bit and then said, "And I guess this, right here, is how you have to come back to the present."

"Yup. It's over too damned quick. Seems stupid to dwell on anything that good. The past is past. I just have to grow up and learn to accept the fact."

Doc: "You probably know what I'm thinking. I'm wondering how the Parts we found figure into all this, if they do."

"Yeah, I know. I've wondered the same thing. Believe it or not, I've actually spoken to them out loud, and asked for help. But so far there's been no response. Well, wait a minute though. Now that we're talking about them, I wonder if that's who is bringing the good memories. They sure pop up more often than they used to. And it's not like I intentionally go looking for them."

Doc: "I'm sure you remember how to contact them in here. At least it might be a way to find out *if* they're involved. Are you up to that?"

"I really don't see why they'd show up here and not at home, but I'll close my eyes and give it a shot." Then a smile crossed his face, and he said, "Well I'll be damned. Fuzzy just said 'Some things you don't want to do alone.' How about that!"

Doc smiled too, and said he agreed completely. He said some people appeared able to do the work on their own, but he never understood how. For himself, he usually needed someone there with him—particularly someone who understood what he was going through. Norm said he felt the same way, and apparently Fuzzy agreed! Then he settled back down, and relaxed. At first the thoughts were all positive, about good times as a child. Then, little by little, he began to feel the old throbbing pain on top of his head. He told Doc about it and complained, "Why the devil is *this* happening? Didn't I suffer through this already? Don't ask me why, but I think Fuzzy is behind this, and I want to ask him a direct question: What the hell are you doing to me, and why are you doing it?"

Norm scowled for a long time, and then heard Fuzzy say, "It's just the first part. Try to stay with it. If you can do that, it should get better. Trust me." Norm reported that, and said out loud, "What the hell do you mean it *should* get better? And how do you expect me to trust you when you're bringing up pain that I've already endured plenty of? Are you my friend or my enemy?"

Doc didn't say anything. He knew Norm remembered what he'd said on the topic, and just kept quiet for a long time. Finally he asked, "Did you get any response to your questions?"

"Just a strange image came to mind. It was a long country road that seemed to run continuously for miles and miles. At first I thought it was going to be another of Mom's games. But then I noticed that the road had a split right in the middle.

A huge gap, like a bomb crater. No way to get from one end to the other. Mom didn't have any games like that."

Doc: "Does the idea of a big gap remind you of anything in your life now?"

"The first thing that comes to mind is what we've been talking about—the gap between the good times and the horrible ones. Is that what you mean?"

Doc said he didn't mean anything specifically. "But that certainly does seem to be a good example. We might be able to get some help here from the inside. Maybe Fuzzy would be able to let us know if we're on the right track."

"Yeah, I wondered about that too. All right, buster, you heard the Doc. What about it?" Almost immediately, Norm heard a single word: close. Norm said out loud, "But no cigar, right?" Again that word: close. I could tell Norm was discouraged, and ready to end the session. But then there was one more word: slow. He told Doc about it.

Doc said, "Well, I'll be! Fuzzy is a smart little dude! But I think there's some worrisome news in there also. It sounds to me like he's telling us this particular issue has to be addressed with caution."

"It's interesting to hear you say that. Having heard his voice a few times, I'm becoming able to read between the lines. There *was* worry, or concern, in there. Okay, buddy, we heard you. Thanks for the warning—sort of."

ENTRY 4:

That same night I asked Fuzzy a question: "Why do you have to keep this a secret from me? Not that I really care all that much, but it's insulting, or something."

"I'm not trying to hurt your feelings, or tease you," he answered. "But I know this is something you and Norm share—this idea that Ted was a mean terrible monster and nothing else. And loosening up that idea is going to take some time, for both of you. There have been so many years of nothing but hate, and well-deserved hate, it will take a major adjustment."

"What do you mean a major adjustment? To *what?* To seeing him as a poor, misunderstood Eagle Scout who just happened to get a lot of bad breaks? Do you want us to just forgive and forget what he did, and how much of Norm's lifetime it has ruined? Are you *crazy?*"

Fuzzy just shook his head slowly and left. I was *steamed*. But I was glad he left. No way

I wanted to be around anybody that nuts. Here I was beginning to trust him, and think maybe he could be a real help in Norm's life. I go to all the trouble to bring back that pain to Norm, and seem to be a little closer to rejoining him in the process, and now Fuzzy is trying to undo everything? Maybe he really *is* crazy! Doesn't sound to me like the kind of help Norm needs!

There was one other thought before I went back to sleep—about misunderstanding. I'm just barely starting to grasp what Doc has said about it, and I wonder if it's part of all this. The idea only stays in my mind for a second or so, and then the hatred of Ted washes it right away. I guess if there's anything true about it it'll come back. Boy, I really need some rest!

ENTRY 5:

Next session, Norm told about another dream. It was about the Civil War.

> "At first I was a Rebel, and then later I switched to being a Yankee. I couldn't tell which side was right, so I'd go back and forth. For some reason, it reminded me of that other dream—about the road with the gap in it. But in that one, there was no way to continue along the road because the gap was so big. But in this

one I went back and forth easily. There *was* a lot of conflict, but I still did it."

Doc: "How does all that relate to your present-day life?"

"The only thing I can connect it with is jumping back and forth between living with my real parents and then Ted and Sadie. I don't understand why I can't stop thinking about it. It almost seems like it's getting obsessive. And I can just hear you thinking, 'Well, then, we probably ought to pay careful attention to it.' Or some such. Is that about right?"

"Mighty close," Doc responded. "So what's your reaction to what I was thinking?"

"I guess my first reaction is I don't *want* to pay close attention to it. It always ends up being painful, and never seems to lead anywhere. It feels like I'm just *stuck*." Fuzzy jumped right in, and very quietly said to Norm, "Right." Just one word again. Norm said out loud, "So it's *you* again!" Somehow, Doc seemed to sense who it was, and Norm told him what he said. Doc asked if he could say any more, but Norm reported that he disappeared. Then he said, "I guess the little bugger is a tease. Or a sadist, one or the other. Why would he do that?"

Doc seemed uncertain. "I don't know at this point. And I agree, it does seem like he's teasing you. But I'll put money on it being necessary, for some reason we don't yet understand."

"Boy, you really have confidence in this guy, don't you!"

Doc: "I've just never met one who intentionally tried to hurt whoever they're part of. I'm not saying it's impossible—it's just something I believe is very rare. I've heard that, in MPD, alters sometimes try to kill others. But it's usually other alters, not the person himself or herself. No, I don't think for a minute Fuzzy is trying to cause you unnecessary pain."

"Well, he may not be trying to kill me, but he sure is pissing me off!"

Doc said he understood that. "I know. I have an idea. How about if we invite him to bring another dream this week, in the hopes that it will shed a bit of light on what's going on?"

At that, Norm's head shook up and down gently, and he said, "Aha! I felt that! You're not so secretive after all!" Then with a bit of a smirk, he added, "And I durn sure could have

99

stopped that, if I'd wanted to." Doc just smiled and said, "No doubt."

ENTRY 6:

I thought a lot about the session, and couldn't resist asking Fuzzy a few questions later. "What is it with you, anyway? You're supposed to be about four years old, but you seem to be way smarter than that. How is that possible?"

"In many ways, I really am four," he said. "I have a lot of the innocence of that age. And a lot of the good memories of Norm's parents. You don't have as many of those because they got buried under all the hate. But believe me, it was just as good as he says it was. It was so good that—"

"Okay, *okay.* I believe you." I was annoyed and had interrupted. "That explains the early part. But what about the smart stuff?"

Fuzzy sighed. "Again, you have to remember that you had a whole lot of pain and hate to deal with, probably a good bit more than me, and that took almost all the energy you had. When you weren't struggling with it, you had to sleep all the time. But not me. I've been awake for a lot more of Norm's life, including when he was in school, and then later in college, so I learned a good bit of stuff along with him. I even know how to drive a car! I hardly ever have to, but it's good to know I can if the need arises. The main difference between you and me is that I'm an optimist and you're a pessimist. I can't say I really understood that until you came out all the way and reminded Norm about the terrible stuff with Ted. I missed a lot of that, mostly because I simply did not want to face it. I knew about part of it, but not the worst part. You'll understand that more as we go along."

Well, that *really* pissed me off! I said, "Dammit! There you go again treating me like a child!"

He just calmly said, "That's only because you *are* one. And that's nothing against you. You've learned ways of helping Norm that I don't know about, or could never do, like getting up in somebody's face when he needs you to. I've seen you do that many times, and applauded you in secret, even though I didn't really know who was doing it. I know there are problems with it, but in the meantime it's very useful to him. Please try to understand what you and Norm are headed for this time is painful in an entirely different way. Try to trust me. You'll be glad you did."

At that point I wished he were more than just a voice—if he'd been flesh and blood I'd have smacked him a good one! Made me so mad and frustrated I just went right to sleep! The very idea: "trust him!" If he's so danged smart he should know that's just about impossible! Now I can't believe I ever *considered* trusting him at all! I hope he falls flat on his face—him and this "different" pain he knows all about!

ENTRY 7:

I didn't even want to be there for the next session. I figured ol' Fuz would be putting on a show, and I wanted no part of it. Sure enough, Norm told about a dream, and I was sure the little smart-ass had brought it.

> "I was back in the Civil War again, but this was different. Each time I would switch back and forth, I would think about the reasons for what I was fighting for. On the one hand, trying to end slavery, which made perfect sense. And then on the other hand, trying to preserve the Southern way of life, and defend my friends and family, who I loved very much! It just about made me crazy trying to figure it out! I'll tell you what this brings to mind, is Maggie saying that Ted sometimes treated her decently, and that she felt 'sorry' for him. And I no sooner say those words out loud than I want to throw up. I could never forget what she said, but it always made me so angry I could never understand it one bit. I mean, he *molested her!* As a grown

man he used her—a young girl—for sexual gratification! How the devil could she feel *sorry* for him? I know we talked about this months ago, and I remember all that. But it hit me different this time for some reason. Yeah, I heard what you said about different 'kinds' of incest, but it still makes my blood boil. Why is that dream making me think about this stuff all over again?"

Doc seemed a little puzzled. "I don't know yet, but it sure does seem like they're connected. You said in the dream it was clear to you that both sides were worth fighting for . . . for different reasons. How does that relate to your life right now, and what you're thinking about?"

"I thought you were going to tell *me*! Oh, forget it. Sniping at you isn't going to help me right now. I'll tell you what amazes me most of all: how crazy mad I get whenever I talk about Ted in any context. How many years has he been in the ground? Do I not understand it's *over*? Is there a Part of me that enjoys the suffering and torment it causes?"

Doc shook his head. "I really doubt that. But let's take the question seriously. Why *would* part of you bring all this up now? Assuming he's not trying to punish you, what could possibly be the point?"

103

Norm seemed to ponder the question for a long time, and then finally said, "Well, I'll be damned. You'll never believe this. Here we are talking about what upsets me the most in my entire life, and my heart is beating out of my chest with rage, and then out of nowhere—it all stops! Can you see it in my face?"

DOC: "It looks more relaxed to me. Why?"

"That's what I mean! My whole body is more relaxed! I feel like I could go to sleep on this couch right now. I've been confused before, but this beats all!"

DOC: "I wonder if some little guy had something to do with it."

"Ha! I just felt the urge to shake my head—but bygod I stopped it! So there, twerp! Now who has the upper hand?"

Doc said he could easily understand why that would irritate Norm, but added, "I still want you to try to believe his real intent is to help you and that he will not cause you any pain that is not absolutely necessary. "

That ended the session, but confused me even more. Okay, so Fuzzy has a lot of power. Big deal. But somehow, Norm has the ability to stop him, at least if he really wants to, or needs to, or just to let him know he can. What? What am I saying? I'm so blasted mixed up I need to sleep—for a long time!

ENTRY 8:

Next thing I know, Norm is having trouble with his boss. Same old crap. Norm is way smarter than he is, so he gets punished for it. It's been going on quite a while, and I figure it's time for me to step in. But then I notice Norm seems to be handling it okay! Finally it's over, and I didn't have to face anybody down. How's that possible? Next session, Norm is talking to Doc about it.

"There we were, for the 50th time, him needling me about nothing in particular, expecting me to bow down to his superior status. But something happened: I didn't bow down! I'm not really sure why. For some reason, I could see that he was the one who was scared, and it calmed me down to the point I didn't have to be so defensive with him. I could actually feel a little bit sorry for him! It feels strange to even say those words out loud, but it's the truth. I could feel Brat there with me, ready to

105

jump right in. But he stayed out of it. I guess he sensed I could handle it on my own. When Big Boss saw his usual strategy wasn't working, he just walked away and left me alone. He did *not* like seeing me feel sorry for him!"

Doc said he was very pleased. "It almost sounds like your brain opened up to some new possibilities, including that your boss might actually be scared of you. Makes perfect sense now, but I wonder why you never thought it before?"

"I wondered exactly the same thing. Once it happened, it made me realize *why* he would be scared of me: he's afraid I'll get his job! And he's dead right—it could happen. He has more seniority than I have, but I'm probably more qualified than he is, especially brain-wise. Truth is, I'm satisfied right where I am, and I don't want the responsibility of supervising other people. At least not right now. Maybe I need to tell him that."

Doc: "Sounds like a winner to me. Wouldn't it be something if the two of you actually got along decently! You might not hate going to work!"

"Now that *is* hard to imagine! But by golly, I'm going to give it a try."

ENTRY 9:

So of course I followed right along with him to work the next day, knowing I still might be needed in a pinch. He caught his boss at the water cooler, and said, "I just wanted you to know something: I like my job just fine. I can see the pressure you're under, and I'm not sure I could handle it as well as you do. So, more power to you. Can we shake on it?"

They did, and Norm just walked away, leaving his boss with a strange look on his face—like for the first time in years he didn't know what to say. He didn't seem mad—just confused. Norm told Kelly about it later. She seemed worried. "Are you sure you're not afraid he'll fire you?"

"No," Norm said. "It wasn't like that. I wasn't mad at him, not like usually. I didn't have to growl at him or get up in his face. I just calmly let him know I wasn't after his job. We shook hands and that was that."

Kelly had trouble believing it could go like that. All these years she'd been terrified he'd get fired for his confrontations, and there was no way the family could get by without him working. So she had to ask one more time, "Are you *sure*?"

"Yeah, I'm sure. Kelly, I know why you're scared. I really understand that. But it was different this time. I think he and I will get along fine now, not having to be afraid of each other. It really should make a difference." Then he did something that alarmed me even more. He held onto her and said, "I love you. Just try to trust me on this one."

So there it was again: "Trust me!" Oh sure, everybody trust everybody! Everything's groovy! No need to be afraid of anything, ever! WHAT? Is everyone nuts? Have all the Teds in the world disappeared? Have the Nazis all had religious conversions? I swear, this whole thing makes me sick. I'm going to sleep. Forever.

ENTRY 10:

Unfortunately, the next session woke me up. Norm was telling Doc about feeling mixed up.

"It's strange. On the one hand, I had this great encounter with my boss, and really believe things will be a little better between us. But at the same time, I feel like I'm about to jump out of my skin! How can that be possible?"

Doc asked, "Did the jumpiness start when you had the encounter with your boss?"

"Yeah, somewhere around there. But that didn't cause it, I know. I came away from that feeling like we had made some progress, and pretty satisfied with how I handled it. I guess I started getting jumpy when I went home and told Kelly what happened. After I got her calmed down, I began to feel all this anxiety, for no reason I can figure."

"Is there anywhere in your body you feel it mostly?" Doc asked.

"Yeah, right in and around my heart. At one point I actually thought I might be having a stroke or heart attack. Now that I'm focusing on it, I'd say it mainly just *hurts*. There is some pressure in there too, but mostly it's pure pain. Is this something you've seen before?"

Doc nodded vigorously. "Yes, I think so. I have a hunch it's connected with the struggles you've been having lately—you know—the Civil War?"

"Okay, maybe you're on to something. But that has always been about indecision and conflict. When did my heart get involved?"

Doc fidgeted around a bit and then said, "I'm guessing some here, but I wonder if maybe the indecision and switching around somehow led up to this—to the heart pain." At that, I could feel Norm's head shake up and down just the slightest bit. Doc asked him, "Did you feel that?"

"Dammit, yes. I felt it start, and tried to stop it. I almost made it, but you noticed. So I guess that means we're dealing with Fuzzy here?"

Doc: "Why don't you ask him?"

Nothing happened for a long while, until finally Norm said, "Yup. It's the little snot."

Doc: "I'm curious. You've always had an affection for him. Why is he 'the snot' now?"

"I feel like he's pushing me now, and I don't like to be pushed. I'll get to stuff when *I'm* ready, not when *he* decides I am."

Doc said that made perfect sense: "I certainly agree with that. Let's see what happens during the week."

I was really glad they both put Fuz in his place. Maybe they'll finally see he's not the smartest guy on the planet, and that he can't just push people around any old way. But one thing bothered me. I could tell I was feeling some of the same heart pain Norm was! Now how the devil did *that* happen? I've always carried that pain on the top of my head, but this heart stuff is new for me. In fact, I guess I never knew if I *had* a heart! Does this mean *I* can have a stroke? What's going on here? Are things ever going to get back to normal?

ENTRY 11:

Next session began with another dream. He told Doc he didn't really want to tell it out loud—there was something about it that was so disturbing he just wanted to forget it. But finally he said, "It was like a still photograph— no action at all. I was holding up a sponge to someone on a cross, like in the Bible. I looked to see who was up there, and it was Ted! Can you imagine how *shocked* I was?"

Doc seemed a little startled himself. "Wow, that IS a shock! How did it make you feel?"

"All sorts of different things. But *bewildered* more than anything! Later I was wondering if maybe Fuzzy is trying to confuse me, or just jerk me around."

Doc: "That doesn't really sound like him, to me. Which gives me an idea.

What about trying to see Ted's face again, like in the dream?"

"Whoa. For some reason that gives me the chills. I'm not sure I'm up to that."

Doc: "How come? What is there to be scared of?"

"Now you're pissing me off. *You* may have nothing to be scared of, but you're not sitting in this chair."

Doc backed off and said, "I'm sorry— you're right. I didn't mean to imply it was going to be easy."

"Oh, what the hell, I'll do it anyway. Just to spite you!"

With that, I could feel Norm grin slightly. But after his breathing slowed way down, he started to twitch a little bit. Doc asked him what that was about.

"I just don't want to do this. Seeing Ted's face in the dream like that was sickening enough. I don't see what good it will do to go through it again." Then he did some heavy breathing, and seemed to relax a bit more. "Oh, mygod. No. This can't be happening."

Doc: "What is it?"

"Ted's face. It's like he's grateful for the water. (Very long pause.) No, that's not possible! Fuzzy, what the hell are you doing this for? Are you deliberately trying to make me crazy? Do you not remember he *hated* me?"

Nobody said anything for a very long time.

Then finally Doc asked softly, "Could both things be possible?"

Norm first wanted to shout at Doc, but then eventually calmed down. He responded so quietly Doc had to get down next to him to be able to hear what he was saying. He said, "I think so. I think I've seen that face before. No, strike that. I KNOW I've seen that face before. I can hear one voice inside me screaming that I'm being played for a fool. Okay, okay, I hear you. But this may be something you just don't know about. Try to hang in there with me on this."

Doc seemed a little confused himself and asked, "On what?"

Norm whispered, "On the face. On whether it was real—and whether maybe he didn't hate me totally all the time. I don't blame you if you're not following this—I'm losing it part of the time too."

Doc: "So the basic question is: Was he ever halfway decent to you at some time, like he was to Maggie?"

"Yes. Exactly. And yes, I could feel my head starting to go up and down, so I'm pretty sure this is Fuzzy's work. I can still hear that other voice trying to get me to throw this out the window, and get back to all the pain and misery he caused. I'm not forgetting for one minute that is all true, but that's not what I'm focused on at the moment. I don't know whether you can tell it or not, but I feel very calm right now. Sort of like before when there was that sudden change. My heart is beating very slowly, and it's not hurting at all. Wow, I wish I could feel this way all the time. But even if that's not likely, it's great to know that this *is* possible, and there is some truth in what's happening. I never in my wildest dreams ever imagined such a thing."

Doc seemed to understand. "That is certainly a huge departure from every-thing else about Ted. We've dealt so much with his cruelty and hatefulness it's hard to conceive of any other side of him. But maybe there really was such a thing. Let's see what comes to you during the week."

Well, that night I screamed at Fuz, "What in the hell are you trying to pull! Are you totally crazy?"

"No, I'm not crazy," Fuzzy insisted. "And I'm not 'pulling' anything that isn't true. Please try to remember there were times in Norm's life when you weren't around. And you had so much pain to deal with you couldn't possibly consider Ted might have had a kinder side—at least for a while."

I asked him what he meant by "for a while."

"Unfortunately, it didn't last," he said and sighed deeply. "As he got older, and Maggie matured into a young woman, his lust took over. Plus, he had always had a mean side to him, and the increased drinking brought that out more. So before long, he began to be the person you remember—and the one you hated as much as he hated you. But I think it's time for you to remember the occasional decency about him also, because it was there. And there's more besides that. You'll see."

I could feel myself tense up and wanted to scream at him to shut up, but he went on anyway, "When you first arrived at his home, you were in dreadful shape. You had just lost your mom and dad, and spent most of the time crying your eyes out. I often wondered if maybe Ted had experienced some loss like that himself, because he seemed to understand what you were going through. And he was actually somewhat patient with you. There were a few times when he would rock you to sleep, and you'll never believe what song he hummed—yes—'The Old Rugged Cross!' He heard you and Maggie doing it and knew it would soothe you. And the look on his face! I'll never forget it. It *was* kindness. Or sympathy, or genuine concern of some sort. No matter how much you hate him, you need to understand things are not as simple as you've always thought. That's why this has taken so long. You've hung on to your hate and bitterness for decades, and for the best of reasons. And I'm not sure those feelings will ever go away completely. He really did some horrible things to you, and it's important to never forget about them. They helped shape you into what you've become, and what Norm has become. But now you know there's more to it, and these new things need to be included also."

Well, I heard every word he said, but to me it was mostly gobbledygook. I got away from him as quickly as I could so I could think about it on my own. He had twisted my mind around so bad I could hardly think at all. Nothing seemed clear anymore. Year after year I had hated Ted for all the misery and pain he caused, and now Fuzzy is suggesting I should *forget* it? Why the devil would I ever want to do such a thing? Next he's going to be telling me how Ted was a sweet little boy who helped lots of old ladies across the street! Well, if he wants to believe Ted is some swell fella, he's welcome to it. Not me. I know too much. Like he himself said, there are plenty of things he *doesn't* know.

ENTRY 12:

On the way to the next session, Norm stopped at Maggie's grave. He knelt down and stroked the headstone, saying, "I really do hope you're happier now. This world seems to have been one misery after another for you." He started to cry, but forced himself to stop. "I just wanted to say to you that the things you told me are starting to make a little more sense. And yet, ironically, I'm more confused than ever! I still hate the memory of Ted just as much as I ever did, but it seems like there's something about him that's eating at me. I just can't put my finger on it. Well, I guess that's all for now. I'll be back soon." As he got up to leave, he thought he heard the word "photos" way off in the distance, but he assumed it was just his imagination, and went on to the car. As he got in and closed the door, the voice sounded nearer, and said distinctly, "Hers." That caused Norm to shudder, mostly because he seemed to understand what it meant. For myself, I hadn't the slightest idea, but I could smell Fuzzy in there somewhere, stirring things up the way he always does.

> When he got to Doc's office, he told about the experience. Doc agreed with me: "Sounds like Fuzzy is telling us something. Any ideas?"

> "Not yet. But I do know there are some of Maggie's things up in our attic. When I get home, I'm going to take a look. Maybe—just maybe—they'll shed some light on all this."

> Doc: "I'm not too sure why I'm saying this, but I would advise you to take it slow. There might be some block-busters up there."

Norm said he would, and left the office more nervous than when he entered.

ENTRY 13:

That night after supper Norm made the much dreaded trip to the attic. After a lot of rummaging around, he found what he was looking for—an entire box filled with Maggie's belongings. He wondered silently why he had never looked in there before, and found himself fumbling so badly opening it that he had to stop and compose himself. When he finally got it open, he suddenly understood why he had such a sense of dread about it: the first photo he saw nearly knocked him down. In a flash, he knew that he had seen it before, but had put it completely out of his mind. It had ceased to exist. It showed Ted in a light Norm had forgotten about entirely. He looked almost like a normal person! He was quite young in the photo—perhaps in his early thirties—and was almost smiling! Norm gasped so loud Kelly heard it, and said from downstairs, "Norm, are you all right?" When he was unable to get any words out, she came up immediately in a panic. He just held the photo out for her to look at. It took her breath away as well. "My God! Is that your Uncle Ted?" Norm just nodded solemnly and said, "I'm afraid so." Kelly went on, "But he looks so . . . so . . . ." "I know," said Norm, breathlessly. "It is, but it can't be. Right now I feel like I'm going stark raving mad. Maybe if I tell you the truth, it will start making things come back to the real world. I've seen that photo before. When I was much younger, before I even met you. But I made it go away; I *put* it away. I guess by that time I had suffered so much at his hand, and hated him so utterly, that I couldn't stand to remember a time when he was different. And it makes me think immediately of what Maggie said about him—that he wasn't always a cruel monster. Wow. This is going to take some time. And I can truly feel a part of me wanting to just burn the damned thing and forget all about it . . . again. But there it is, in real life. And obviously there are more in there, probably some similar to this." At that, he thumbed through a few more, but said nothing. "Okay, that's enough for now. I also understand now why Doc suggested I go slow with this. He seemed to have some inkling about what I might find. Know what? I need a beer!"

ENTRY 14:

Next session Norm was telling Doc about looking through Maggie's possessions. He said he found a photo that seemed impossible.

> NORM: "I still can't believe what I saw in there. There was a photo of Ted when we first got to their home, and it knocked me for a loop. Ted looked way different from how I remember him. The snarl was gone from his face, and the bitterness too. He almost looked like a normal human being!" It took him a long time before he said: "He was smiling!"

Doc: "Man that *is* a surprise! How did you react to it?"

"I was absolutely dumbfounded. I barely looked at a few others, and at first thought the photo must have been doctored, but then I remembered they couldn't do such things in those days. So the picture was *real.* I kept going through more and more of them, hoping to find one of him as I remember him, to bring me back to reality. There weren't a whole lot of them—maybe five or six—but they all looked the same. He and Sadie both looked like ordinary people! Not only that, but you could see some concern in their faces for me and Maggie."

Well, there were plenty of times in Norm's sessions when I just drifted off and went to sleep, and I tried as hard as I could this time, believe me. But it didn't work. There's an irritating part of me that demands to know the truth, and it kept me wide awake. Dammit.

Doc was a bit dumbfounded. "I have to say I did not see this coming! It seemed real clear that Ted and Sadie were bad, evil people, and that was that. But this brings a lot of things into question."

"I know! My head is still swimming around like crazy, and I feel totally unbalanced. But I know those photos don't lie, and I have no choice but to pay attention to what they're telling me. Right away it makes me think back to Maggie's saying she felt sorry for Ted. Maybe she wasn't a wacko after all. Maybe she saw a side of him I never did."

"I'm a little curious as to why you didn't bring the photos in here with you," Doc wondered out loud.

"I know. I thought about it, but just could not do it. It's one thing for me to see them, and another for you to see them, and then have to deal with *your* reactions. I wasn't quite ready for that. But I will bring them in next time. At least I'll try."

ENTRY 15:

Needless to say, my head was swirling just as bad as Norm's. I made myself look at the photos at the same time he did. It was all I could do not to turn away from them. I just kept saying "They're lies! They're lies!" But something inside me knew better. At first it almost made me sick, but I finally settled down and looked squarely at them, and I saw the same things Norm saw: a couple of more-or-less decent people. I found myself looking everywhere for an explanation that would allow me to preserve all my old hate and rage, but nothing worked. I realized slowly that I would have to change some of those ideas: they were not the whole truth. It was as though the world as I knew it was coming to an end, and would never be the same.

I hated going to the next session, because I was sure Norm would bring the photos with him. He did, and Doc confirmed my worst suspicions: he saw the same thing Norm did. And me too, sorry to say. There was Ted minus the hateful look, almost like he was trying to offer support. And Sadie even looked kindly toward Maggie, like she had some idea of what she'd been through.

Finding the photos made Norm recall some folders containing Maggie's writing. He had never looked at them, for obvious reasons, but chose to do so now. Against my better judgment, I looked at them with him. This is what they said:

Dear Diary:

I'm eleven now. Norm and I have been here for about four years. Time goes so slow when you're miserable! At first it wasn't so bad. Ted and Sadie were not at all happy about having to take us when Mom and Dad were killed, but they agreed. We actually had some pretty good times. Ted knew some of the same games our real parents played, and every now and then we'd have fun playing them. There were even a few times he would sing "The Old Rugged Cross" to help us go to sleep. He and Sadie didn't have any extra money, and we had to do lots of chores to make ends meet, but we knew there was no choice. There was never enough to eat, and Ted always seemed to grab up the most. Sadie never did anything to stop him, and we knew better than to say one word. He won't let Sadie work, even though he doesn't really make enough money for four people to live on. She's scared to death of him, even though he never beats her or anything. I guess he must steal all the beer he drinks, because there's no way he could pay for all that.

I've begged and begged Sadie to stop Ted from beating on Norm.

She just tells me to hush, and always says there's a lot I don't know about him. That he wasn't always this way, but going to war in Vietnam changed him in really bad ways. He sometimes beats on Norm pretty bad, especially when he's drunk, but I get in the way and beg him to stop. He always says he will, but never does, or only until the next time. I know very well how mean he is to Norm, but I also know a lot of it is because he's so miserable himself! I've asked him about how he grew up, but he won't tell me anything at all, so that's no help. And if I bring up the war he just goes into a rage. Despite everything, I feel sorry for him. Norm thinks I'm crazy to feel that way, but I do. I can't help it. I guess I might feel different if it was me he was beating on. Norm scares me sometimes. When Ted is especially rough on him, I've seen his eyes glaze over, like he was getting ready to have a seizure or something. For a while afterward, he doesn't even talk right. Something is wrong, I can tell, and I hate that I can't fix it!

Later:

I just turned fifteen. Things are much worse. A few months ago, Sadie told me about Ted when he was in the Army, about six years ago. He had said it was a way to provide more money, but I think he just wanted to get away. He did send some money home, but it wasn't really any better. He finally got an honorable discharge and came back. She said something happened to him over there, in a place called Vietnam. Something terrible. She says he will never talk about it, but from his nightmares, she can tell he was in some sort of prison camp, apparently for a very long time. Now, almost every night I can hear his blood-curdling screams coming from the bedroom. Just occasionally I can make out some words, and it sounds like he's being tortured. Sadie just runs out of the room and comes in and sleeps with us. I feel terrible for him. Whatever happened made him a different person. Not that he was ever really kind or anything, but he was never as mean as he is now. He gets drunk a lot more often, and can't hold a decent job. Every time he gets fired he gets that much meaner.

And that's not the worst of it. He'd better not find this, because he said if I ever told he'd kill me and Norm together. But, he does stuff to me. I dare not write it down, but it's real bad. He always says it isn't, and how it's normal and everything, and how it's proof that he cares about me, but I know it's not. It makes me sick. It didn't at first, but then it got more and more painful, and he didn't seem to care at all when I cried. It got to where he would cover my mouth so I couldn't scream. Now, in my sleep, I clench my teeth so bad they're starting to crack. I try to stop doing it, but I can't. He's so mean to me and Norm that I just hope he disappears, or gets put in jail or something. The strange thing is, when I hear his screams in the *night, I still can't help but feel sorry for him. He's like a wounded animal. How can your heart not hurt for someone like that? I've tried to tell Norm about it, but he just hates him, plain and simple. I don't blame him at all.*

ENTRY 16:

Norm took the diary with him to the next session, and held it out for Doc to read. When he finished it, I could tell Doc was exhausted. He just put it down and took a very deep breath and then finally started talking.

Doc: "Good Lord. This sure puts things in a different light. I guess I always assumed that *something* terrible happened in his life for him to treat you like he did, and this sure helps to nail it down. I remember something my grandfather told me years ago that I've learned to appreciate: 'There are two types of people in the world—those who have been to war and those who haven't.' That pretty well sums it up. You and I can be forever grateful for being among 'those who haven't.'"

"I know, and I agree completely. It sure helps me to have a touch of compassion for him, which I'll readily admit was entirely missing previously. But, even allowing for all that, I still have a couple of questions. First, because some men go through things like prison camp and don't necessarily turn into angry beasts, what made him different? And second, what about molesting Maggie? I don't see that the war experiences would have to have made him into a pedophile. Or is there a connection I'm not seeing?"

Doc: "No, not that I know of. I think one of the things this teaches us is that there is a lot about him we will probably never know. Lots and lots of very bad stuff. Still, I think knowing *some* of it is a big step toward understanding the whole situation better, and being able to forgive him a little bit."

"It's amazing to me. Year after year there was this vicious hatred, and then suddenly I see these pictures and read her diary, and everything is a little different! I mean, not entirely. I'll never forget how he hurt me—and her. But when I really looked closely at the pictures, I could feel something change inside me. A sort of softening—like my heart had been holding on to that hate with a death grip, and was finally able to loosen it a bit. (After several minutes.)

I believe that Ted was, in the final analysis, an anguished, bitter man most of his life. And he caused some serious damage. But I have to ask myself: could I have done much better? I'm truly not sure. He *did* help us both out for a while, and when he no longer could, he became more and more of a monster. I imagine he hated himself about as much as I hated him. I can remember now that he never seemed to 'enjoy' hitting me, and hardly ever did it when he was sober. Unfortunately, that wasn't much of the time. (Long sigh.) I'll tell you something else that feels strange: I'm wondering where I'll get my energy now. I think I fed off that hate for so many years I wonder what there will be to take its place. I guess I'll find out soon enough."

DOC: "Yes, I guess you will. I just keep thinking about Maggie, and how this conflict must have been in some ways even worse for her. I guess it may have actually killed her."

"I know. Me too. I remember when they found Ted dead in his bed, she wailed like it was her that was dying. I couldn't imagine why. Myself—I thought it was the best thing that ever happened. But she apparently never forgot his good side, despite everything he did to her. That's pretty amazing in itself. She was the most soft-hearted person I ever knew, and maybe it wound up killing her. But she could only feel what she felt, and nothing I ever said changed that. Nor should it have, I suppose.

Doc: "I know, for some people the caring simply will not die, no matter what."

"She sure seems to have been one of those. Well, Doc, I guess that does it for now. I'm sure you know how much I appreciate your help. I hope I won't need you again, but if I do I'll sure be glad you're here." He reached out to shake Doc's hand, but surprised himself by opening his arms to give him a big hug! Doc seemed happy to get it.

When he got home, Kelly wanted to know all about it. Even though Norm was still pretty worn out, he told her the whole story. When he was done, she said if she ever met Doc, she might be inclined to hug him as well. After some silence, Norm said, "You know, I think one of the most important things I got out of the whole business was learning to trust myself. Earlier, there were so many things I did that either I was only half aware of or thought were just plain crazy, and none of it made any sense to me. I used to hate myself for crying so often, when it felt like a baby doing it. But once I understood that the tears were due to legitimate feelings—and pain I had made myself forget about—I didn't hate it anymore. Now, crying is something I actually value and an ability I hope to never lose."

Kelly nodded vigorously and said, "I know what you mean. And what a relief it is to me to not want to punish you for it anymore!"

Norm put his arm around her. "It's just that you didn't understand it any more than I did. I don't blame you at all. Or myself for that matter!"

ENTRY 17:

Not much need for me to add anything more, except to say things really are better for Norm. Not that he is never depressed or anything, because he does get that way sometimes. I guess life is no cakewalk for anybody. Kelly and the boys seem to like him better, and that means a lot to him. He still has some trouble with his boss, but he doesn't stay upset about it for days like he used to. Oh yeah, and he plays hackysack with his boys a little more. He's even getting back some of his old form, as he's quick to remind them. Seems like a very good thing.

Fuzzy and I agree that we're still not entirely back inside Norm, and maybe that will never happen. But it feels so much better to be closer, and for him to know we're both here if he needs us, it doesn't seem to matter as much.

I still find the whole thing hard to believe. Or at least I did, until I looked at those pictures and read the diary with him. I guess Fuzzy remembered them the whole time. He and I don't talk much anymore—there's not really much need to. We both know what we feel, and we both know we're right to feel differently. That's just the way it is. Norm would be crazy to forget either one of us, and probably couldn't even if he wanted to. Sometimes he leans a little more toward one of us than the other, but we know he values us both and will never forget what we brought back to him. It was *all* true.

Acknowledgment

My thanks to Micki: my editor, my consultant and my friend. Your untiring perseverance and enthusiasm have been the greatest help to me. I could never have done it without you. I hope to be able to offer similar help with your book.

www.ingramcontent.com/pod-product-compliance
Lightning Source LLC
Chambersburg PA
CBHW070807280326
41934CB00012B/3096